Enhancing Aesthetic Reac
and Response

Enhancing Aesthetic Reading and Response

Philip M. Anderson
Queens College of the City University
of New York

Gregory Rubano
Toll Gate High School
Warwick, Rhode Island

National Council of Teachers of English
1111 Kenyon Road, Urbana, Illinois 61801

Staff Editor: David A. Hamburg

Cover Design: Michael J. Getz

Interior Design: Tom Kovacs for TGK Design

NCTE Stock Number 15616-3050

Library of Congress Cataloging-in-Publication Data

Anderson, Philip M.
    Enhancing aesthetic reading and response / Philip M. Anderson. Gregory Rubano.
        p.   cm.
    Includes bibliographical references (p.).
    "NCTE stock no. 15616-3050"—T.p. verso.
    ISBN 0-8141-1561-6
    1. Reader-response criticism.   2. Reading—United States.
I. Rubano, Gregory, 1949–   . II. Title.
PN98.R38A54   1991
801'.95—dc20   91–21331
                                                         CIP

Contents

Acknowledgments

The following people contributed ideas, exercises, or examples: Ascher Rivlin, James Squire, Nathan S. Blount, Bonnie Sunstein, Kristin Dittmann, Robin Feingold, Suzann McKiernan, Elizabeth Masciale, James Silvia, Steven Varrichio, Brian Schwegler, Beth Wissler, Charles Gaffney, Justine Clayton, Sun Ahn, Kevin Smith, Michelle Lemoi, Allison Werb, Yomana Sukkar, Stephanie Carlsten, Chris Thompson, Dan Tessier, Jim Stilgenbauer, and Peter Loring.

Grateful acknowledgment is made to the following poets, their representatives, and publishers for permission to reprint copyrighted material: "We Never Know How High." Reprinted by permission of the publishers and the Trustees of Amherst College from *The Poems of Emily Dickinson,* Thomas H. Johnson, ed., Cambridge, Mass.: The Belknap Press of Harvard University Press, Copyright 1951, © 1955, 1979, 1983 by the President and Fellows of Harvard College. "The Eagle" by Alfred, Lord Tennyson, from *Poems of Tennyson.* Jerome Buckley (Ed.). Riverside Edition. Boston: Houghton Mifflin, 1958. "Death." Reprinted with permission of Macmillan Publishing Company from *The Poems of W.B. Yeats: A New Edition* edited by Richard J. Finnernan. Copyright 1933 by Macmillan Publishing Company, renewed 1961 by Bertha Georgie Yeats. "The Choice." From *Not So Deep as a Well* by Dorothy Parker. Copyright 1936, renewed (c) 1964 by Dorothy Parker. Used by permission of Viking Penguin, a division of Penguin Books USA Inc. "War Is Kind." From *The Works of Stephen Crane: Volume X, Poems and Literary Remains,* edited by Fredson Bowers. Originally published by the University Press of Virginia, Charlottesville, Virginia, 1975. "When I Heard the Learn'd Astronomer" by Walt Whitman, from *Complete Poetry and Selected Prose.* James E. Miller (Ed.). Riverside Edition. Boston: Houghton Mifflin, 1959.

1 Theory and Research

Poetry is a search for the inexplicable.
 —Wallace Stevens

Introduction

Reports from the National Assessment of Educational Progress over the last twenty years have consistently suggested that U.S. students are quite competent in literal-level comprehension skills. On the other hand, these same students are not as skillful at inferential reasoning and other higher-order thinking skills needed for more sophisticated reading (Purves, 1984). One commonly heard explanation of this problem is that students are not taught higher-order reading and thinking skills. But it might also be that students are being taught to read in ways which will not result in the higher-level abilities we wish for them, especially in the reading of literature.

Currently, students are actually taught to prize literal comprehension over other types of reading and thinking because, instead of promoting creative and aesthetic responses to literature, schools have employed "comprehension" models from developmental reading. Comprehension models assume that literal comprehension occurs prior to higher-order reasoning and creative response, and therefore these models treat texts in an analytical, generally reductive fashion.

Reporting on the state of reading instruction in the landmark 1977 National Society for the Study of Education Yearbook, *The Teaching of English*, Margaret Early declares that "intuition and experience suggest that some of the skills emphasized by reading teachers (e.g., finding the main idea, subordinating details to main ideas, SQ3R, summarizing and outlining) have little pertinence to reading much of literature" (Early, 1977, p. 193). Indeed, emphasis on comprehension has transformed literature study from an activity aimed at enriching the linguistic and experiential background of our students to one concerned with remembering and reiterating the content of stories, poems, and novels. Hirsch's cultural literacy model, a newly popular vision of literary

1

study drawn from the most recent general reading research, maintains that memorizing cultural facts is a prerequisite to reading literature (Hirsch, 1988).

Probably of more concern to English teachers is the finding from the International Association for the Evaluation of Educational Achievement (IEA) that U.S. students tend to assume a "moralistic interpretive response stance" when reading and responding to literature (Galda, 1982, p. 119). In addition, students tend to concentrate on content, rather than form (probably a legacy of comprehension instruction), in responding (117). Even more disturbing, it was the higher-achieving students in that study who exhibited the fewest different kinds of response, not their lower-achieving counterparts. Based on this finding, and on other clues in the data from the IEA assessment, Purves claims that students have probably been "taught that certain responses and only certain responses are appropriate" in school (Purves, with Harnisch, Quirk & Bauer, 1981, p. 89).

Of course, when not emphasizing reading comprehension in school, the model for literary study has been the New Criticism. A dominant force in literary thinking for the last half-century, the New Criticism puts a premium on finding the "objective," authoritative meaning of the text. In addition, the moralistic tradition in literature study that preceded New Criticism never really left the classroom, leaving the legacy of students searching the text for the moral of the narrative, usually articulated as a "theme" statement. The literature curriculum has acquired an analytical and moralistic frame, with little time left for the aesthetic and creative aspects of literary reading. Schools assume the premises of both these approaches to the detriment of literature study, aesthetic reading, and our students' aesthetic response.

Interest in redefining literary reading in schools dates back at least to the 1938 original publication of Louise Rosenblatt's *Literature as Exploration* (Rosenblatt, 1983). In refining her early work, Rosenblatt has proposed the notion of "aesthetic" and "efferent" psychological stances that readers assume while reading a text (Rosenblatt, 1978). Efferent reading (from the Latin word "effere," meaning "to carry away") is concerned primarily with information gained from the text, while aesthetic reading is concerned primarily with the "lived-through" experience of the text. (Rosenblatt will be discussed at length later.)

SQ3R and many other reading strategies are really aimed at the efferent stance in reading; what the student remembers for reiteration on a test of "story or information recall" becomes the aim of instruction. Much of the reading instruction in schools is aimed at efferent reading, usually at the expense of aesthetic reading. Since the appropriate psychological stance for reading a literary text is the aesthetic stance, literary experience, and even the literature curriculum itself, can be shortchanged in a curriculum based on efferent reading.

An efferent reading focus can also create problems with regard to teaching materials and texts. Since aesthetic reading and experience are not primary considerations in the development of reading texts and support materials, efferent forms of reading are frequently promoted by available teaching materials. Reading comprehension tests, with their emphases on remembering and analyzing text, also promote efferent forms of reading. Literary texts are often presented to students as if the primary task of a reader is to memorize the text or carry away cultural information from the text. The ultimate abuse of this trend results in the infamous "What facts does this poem teach you?" question that Rosenblatt found in an elementary reading text (Rosenblatt, 1980).

Most generalized reading strategies were developed for use with expository prose and do not work as well, or at all, with stories and poems. The current school literature curriculum appears to tout *Huckleberry Finn* as a book that many people have enjoyed over the last one hundred or so years because they all liked the "main idea." Or worse, schools promote the idea that anyone who does not comprehend the author's theme of individual conscience in an unjust society could not have enjoyed, or benefited from, the experience of reading the book.

The view of reading present in the schools remains a key factor for promoting aesthetic reading and response. If we believe that reading is solely getting meaning from a text, a meaning that is "correct" or sanctioned by authority, then the curriculum emphasis will continue to be centered on the efferent response. But even if we believe that at least half the task of reading literature is efferent, and that analysis and memory objectives are appropriate to much of the literature curriculum, we still need to evoke creative and aesthetic responses to fulfill the rest of the objectives of the literature curriculum.

As for testing the reading of literature, the ingredient most often lacking is questions that assess student ability to respond aesthetically. This is somewhat ironic, given the stress put on the construction of meaning in recent mainstream reading research (Davidson, 1988). Constructivist views of reading require some sort of aesthetic and creative response on the part of the reader. Thus the aesthetic response is expected of our students, but it is rarely taught and rarely sought from them.

Aesthetic Form and Cognitive Development

One of the principal questions regarding the promotion of aesthetic reading and reasoning in schools is whether efferent reading is a prerequisite to aesthetic reading. The misconception persists that one cannot read aesthetically until one can read analytically for comprehension of the text. While this idea appears commonsensical on its face, research demonstrates that analytical ability does not antedate creative ability developmentally, nor does efferent reading necessarily precede aesthetic reading.

Howard Gardner and his associates' research on child development cites the fascinating case of metaphor use: metaphor production precedes metaphor comprehension developmentally (Gardner, 1982, p. 166). In addition, Gardner maintains that no additional cognitive development is necessary after the age of seven for continued artistic growth (p. 213). Gardner and his associates found that children are less concerned with content than generally believed when approaching a literary text:

> We approach and evaluate artwork in terms other than those of simple realism. Consideration of composition, expressivity, and the elaboration of detail and texture . . . contribute significantly to our assessment of the merits of the work. (p. 76)

Even little children are artistic in their initial assumptions about literary texts.

A well-known example of aesthetic response to literature at an early age comes from Kenneth Koch's work with elementary school students. His descriptions of reading and writing poetry with children demonstrate that children can respond to literary experience through aesthetic forms of language (Koch, 1990). Koch's approach is especially intriguing because students respond to poems by writing poems, i.e., they respond to literature by writing literature.

Arthur Applebee's research shows children as young as two years telling rudimentary stories, i.e., applying an aesthetic function to language use (Applebee, 1978). If metaphor production can precede comprehension, if toddlers can tell stories for the sake of storytelling, and if fourth graders can write poems about poems, aesthetic reading and response can certainly proceed without first attending to teaching literal comprehension to adolescents.

Another curriculum question frequently raised asks whether aesthetic experience is necessary at all, or is only an educational and social "frill." Implicit in the question is the assumption that aesthetic concerns are primarily covered by affective or emotive objectives rather than cognitive ones. Actually, most theory and research in creative and aesthetic development emphasize aesthetic rationality or aesthetic cognition. Many researchers and theorists agree with Maxine Greene's point of view that "aesthetic experiences are not only affective and intuitive, . . . they involve persons perceptually and cognitively as much as they do emotionally" (Greene, 1981; Greene, 1982, p. 327). On the other hand, one of the defining factors of this type of cognitive research is that it implicitly accounts for affective response. In other words, the cognitive dimension is studied in the context of the affective.

Two highly influential language researchers suggest that social context is essential to learning learning, and that aesthetic learning is a crucial aspect of language and cognitive development. Lev Vygotsky's research into the nature of language development clearly demonstrates that linguistic and cognitive development of adolescents is dependent on the social environment in which they learn language (Vygotsky, 1962).

And, according to James Britton, the aesthetic and creative functions of language are essential to psycholinguistic development. He theorizes that individuals, within a social context, construct a representation of the world through language. A necessary part of this worldview construction engages aesthetic functions and forms of language (Britton, 1976).

Britton's conclusions from his studies of language development argue for the necessity of the "special form of dialogue that is carried on between writer and readers of a work of literature" (Britton, 1976, p. 29). The students' language development is enhanced by approaching the text in a dialogical and aesthetic manner. Louise Rosenblatt's essential argument that reading is a transaction between reader and text, a dialogical model of reading, is in accordance with the psycholinguistic research.

Britton also claims that literary reading is a "principal means to individuation" in adolescence (Britton, 1970, p. 265). In light of Britton's theories, the transactional view of reading proposed by Rosenblatt becomes a central fact in the psycholinguistic development of the individual language learner. Without opportunities for aesthetic language experience in school, adolescents will be limited in their ability to respond to literature in an aesthetic manner.

Aesthetic reading usually occurs in spite of the school environment, either by students who read extensively outside classroom readings or in unvoiced experience during school reading. The ability to assume an aesthetic stance in out-of-school reading is hinted at in the research finding that students are more likely to finish books chosen from the library than books assigned in class (Purves & Beach, 1972, p. 103). The prevalent belief in this instance speculates that students read books whose content "interests" them, and it is this "interest" that accounts for the phenomenon. Yet it is also possible that students who freely choose books adopt an aesthetic stance toward the text, which in turn, produces a desirable aesthetic experience.

English language arts teachers can nurture an aesthetic environment—and promote aesthetic forms of reading and thinking within it—for all students. Structuring aesthetic experience requires appropriate theoretical framing and methodological procedure in the classroom. For students to respond to literature in aesthetic ways, they need instructional situations allowing them consideration of form as well as content. Thus classroom activities need to value image and emotion as well as plot analysis and intellect.

Without an aesthetic environment and teacher sponsorship of an aesthetic stance toward reading, students will not employ it in school reading. As a result, many students never approach literature study in an aesthetic fashion, even though it is the primary manner in which educated readers are expected to read literature.

Generally, the deck is stacked against aesthetic reading in schools, from basal readers to comprehension tests. Every subject except English emphasizes efferent reading, especially through textbook reading, and the English class only contributes to the problem when it emphasizes reading comprehension or the efferent stance in reading literature. The efferent approach implicit in comprehension instruction sends a message to students that they can never read in an aesthetic manner or respond fully to literature because there is always something they do not understand, something beyond their "comprehension." Literary works promise aesthetic events as well as ideas and values; aesthetic reading is a necessary part of the literary experience.

Reader-Response Theories

Principal investigations into the reading of literary texts have not generally been explored in traditional reading research as they have been in research and theoretical studies concerning response to literature, i.e., "reader-response" studies. Reader-response theorists (both psychological and textual) are primarily concerned with the reader's interaction with, and response to, a text. To literary theorists, the debate is whether the reader or the text is the primary influence.

As Emrys Evans, citing Rosenblatt, declares, reader-response theorists tend to think of the text as "a *constraint* on the reader's activity, rather than as a *norm* which everyone should try to approach in the same way" (Evans, 1987, p. 27, emphasis in original). In any case, the theoretical center (and, therefore, the teaching focus) of reader response is the point at which the reader interacts with the text. Reader response investigates the interaction of text and reader, the affective and cognitive processes of understanding and enjoyment.

Though I. A. Richards's study, *Practical Criticism* (1929, discussed below), has exerted the most influence on the methodology of response research, Rosenblatt's transactional theory has shaped the assumptions and emphases of most reader-response research. Her basic view of the relationship between the reader and the text forms the core of most modern studies of literary response. Drawing on Dewey and Bentley's transactional psychology, Rosenblatt insists on the term "transaction" to describe the reading act. She argues that the word "interaction" evolves from a mechanistic tradition, based on a machine metaphor, while transaction "designates an ongoing process in which the elements or parts are seen as aspects or phases of a total situation" (Rosenblatt, 1985, p. 98).

The aesthetic and creative criteria of such research are exemplified in her statement that "fundamentally, the process of understanding a work implies a re-creation of it" (Rosenblatt, 1983, p. 113). As David Bleich acknowledges, "Rosenblatt's thinking represents the formulation, for the first time, of an intellectual attitude that can accommodate response, in its full dimensions, in the organized study of literature" (Bleich, 1978, p. 109). Unfortunately, a crucial theoretical insight, the postulation of aesthetic and efferent reading stances, has been given little attention in the research literature.

Rosenblatt's theories developed over forty years, beginning in 1938 with the Progressive Education Association–sponsored book *Literature as Exploration* (Rosenblatt, 1983). Central to the concern here from those early investigations are her assertions, drawn from John Dewey, among others, of the importance of "constructive thinking," and the belief that "reason should arise in a matrix of feeling" (pp. 226–227). Rosenblatt championed students' personal response to literature and the idea that the reader and the text together create the literary experience (p. 66). In a "coda" to *Literature as Exploration* written in 1966, after reminding us that "no one else can read a literary work for us," she argues that "the benefits of literature can emerge only from creative activity on the part of the reader" (p. 278). As for the responsibility of teachers of literature, it is to "keep alive this view of the literary work as personal evocation, the product of creative activity carried on by the reader under the guidance of the text" (p. 280).

Rosenblatt's 1978 book *The Reader, the Text, the Poem* further develops the notion of the aesthetic transaction, citing complementary research carried on during the intervening years. Most important, Rosenblatt differentiates between two fundamental purposes of reading, which she labels "aesthetic" and "efferent." She asserts that readers assume a psychological stance in relation to text, either an aesthetic stance, concerned with cognitive and affective responses during the actual reading event, or an efferent stance, concerned with what the reader carries away from the text.

According to Rosenblatt, reading activity occupies a continuum between aesthetic and efferent stances. At the extreme efferent end of the continuum, the reader is disengaged from personal and qualitative response; the reader focuses on retaining information and concepts after the experience of reading. On the aesthetic end of the continuum, the reader's attention is focused on the reading event itself, invoking primarily personal and qualitative response (p. 27).

Most readers will adopt each stance variably during the reading of a text, though the emphasis remains on one or the other (p. 37). A reader could read *Moby Dick* solely in an efferent manner, or could read instructions for putting together a bicycle entirely in an aesthetic manner. While both situations are possible, neither would be very profitable. Certainly, aesthetic reading and aesthetic forms of thinking may be appropriately applied in nonliterary situations, such as reading and writing metaphorically in science or biography (Rubano & Anderson, 1988; Sunstein & Anderson, 1989). But the aesthetic reading stance is necessary to literary reading; the psychological stance, not the text by itself, determines the aesthetic experience of the literary text.

Since any text may be read either efferently or aesthetically, the social context of reading can be a determining factor of stance (Rosenblatt, 1978, p. 25). Rosenblatt suggests that the adoption of stance is dependent on the sociophysical setting (p. 78), meaning that the reading situation, the aim of the school lesson, for instance, will determine the stance. It becomes the English teacher's responsibility to create an environment in which aesthetic response can occur (Hynds, 1989).

Though some efferent and aesthetic reading activity occurs while reading all texts, the issue is always one of primary emphasis. Unfortunately, as Rosenblatt claims, "In our schools, the emphasis in the teaching of reading is almost entirely on the efferent stance" (1978,

p. 79). Rosenblatt, herself, recommends eliminating efferent questions entirely from school literary experiences (Rosenblatt, 1980, p. 392). Such a move to the aesthetic end of the spectrum, however, takes an effort of will and technique on the part of the English teacher.

Asking students questions that focus on literal comprehension of a text promotes an efferent stance toward the reading situation. Asking, "What is this type of poem called?" about a Shakespearean sonnet, or "What is the name of the King of Scotland?" does not promote aesthetic reading. But, "Which character in *Hamlet* did you like to hear speak?" or "What did you see when Ophelia committed suicide?" can promote an aesthetic reading stance. The instructional situation created by the teacher can limit, or even eliminate, the aesthetic transaction. Literature lessons therefore must be framed by the appropriate questions and activities, those that establish an aesthetic stance to the text.

Two key points in Rosenblatt's theory are of the most interest here: (1) the reader and text together create the literary experience, and (2) the aesthetic experience occurs during the reading of the text, but only through an aesthetic cognitive stance. Literary texts do not produce the literary experience; they merely guide the constructive reader who has adopted an aesthetic stance toward the text. Simply providing a literary text does not guarantee that students will read it aesthetically.

In recent years, reader-response criticism has gained some prominence in literary scholarship. Iser (1978) and Bleich (1978) produced influential books on the role of the reader in the interpretation of a text, and theirs were followed by two influential collections of reader-response criticism, edited by Suleiman and Crosman (1980) and Tompkins (1980), respectively. Indeed, divisions exist among reader-response theorists as to the exact nature of the aesthetic transaction, each assigning a greater or lesser role to constraints of the text. But there is general agreement among these theorists that reading and interpretation models or theories that do not account for the role of the reader in creating the literary experience, or the affective and cognitive response of the reader in reading, are not adequate for a theory of literary reading. In fact, Alan Purves claims that "the reader has come to replace the text as the central figure in the literary enterprise" (Purves, 1985).

Earlier studies, typified by I. A. Richards's, place more value on the text than on the reader, and recent trends, represented by Bleich, put more emphasis on the reader than on the text. The key shift in approaches to theories of reading literature during the last sixty years is the move from a primarily efferent stance, in which the reader is subservient to the text and its purported meanings, to an aesthetic stance, in which the reader is an active participant in the creation of literary meaning and aesthetic linguistic experience.

Of all the reader-response models, Rosenblatt's model is most concerned with educational applications. Her model functions so effectively in the classroom because of the value it places on both text and reader, coupled with its distinction between efferent and aesthetic reading. The current situation in schools runs the gamut of text-centered to subjective approaches, while efferent reading stances are endorsed by reading comprehension instruction. Rosenblatt's theory carries the most transformative and explanatory power for the class-room.

Rosenblatt's theoretical insights have gained more relevance recently as a result of various efforts to provide literary texts for reading instruction at all levels of reading instruction (Squire, 1989). Merely introducing literary texts into a reading program based on efferent reading strategies will not improve literary reading. Instead, applying efferent techniques to literature instruction will probably result in even worse efferent readers who, in addition, find literary texts baffling, boring, or useless.

As Rosenblatt reminds us, "the literary work is not primarily a document in the history of language or society. . . . As a work of art, it offers a special kind of experience" (Rosenblatt, 1983, p. 278). The neglect of this "special kind of experience" in school instruction could produce readers who think the primary task in reading *Oliver Twist* is to learn about social conditions in early Victorian England, the primary interest in reading Hemingway is to learn about killing animals and humans, or the essential motive for reading *The Color Purple* is self-discovery through race or gender identification.

Research in Reader Response

Research in reader response is generally concerned with the nature of reading and response (especially the educational implications) as op-posed to reader-response criticism's interest in normative readings of a text. Whereas reader-response critics are interested in the relationship of the reader and the text in the interpretation of a text, response researchers are primarily concerned with the linguistic and psycholog-ical aspects of reading and responding to a text. The distinction is important if only to highlight the differences between the interests of critics and the interests of teachers.

There are two main categories of research on reading literature and responding to literature:

1. *Research that examines the written or oral responses of readers produced during, or directly after, the reading of the text.* This type of research is generally called "protocol analysis" research because the researcher analyzes written or spoken protocols produced by the respondents. Readers articulate their thoughts and feelings in the protocols.

2. *Research that provides response opportunities not tied to articulating a response in speech or writing, but through other structured means.* This type of research is generally called "passive ability" research, and seeks to record the unarticulated responses of readers.

Both types of research provide insights into aesthetic reading and response and also suggest useful classroom strategies for evoking and teaching aesthetic reading and response.

Articulated Response

Articulated response research really began in 1929 with the publication of I. A. Richards's *Practical Criticism* (Richards, 1962). Richards used protocol analysis as his research methodology, a method still common to most of the research in the field. Generally, readers' written or oral response protocols are analyzed by researchers to investigate various characteristics of the responders or the articulated response. Protocol analysis research has elicited significant insights into child and adolescent reading behavior, and some of the more influential studies concerning literature study in schools (K–12) have used the method.

The primary mode of literary response used in classrooms, writing literary essays and writing personal responses to texts, is reinforced by protocol analysis research. Research using protocol analysis does not focus on reading comprehension or interpretation exclusively, nor is there any inherent reason that written or spoken protocols must focus on comprehension or interpretation. But its methodology of articulating response, combined with the school's emphasis on reading tests and reading research's emphasis on comprehension, does tend to focus student attention on written or spoken reiteration, representing the "comprehension" or "interpretation" of the literary work. And since protocols are generally written as essays or expressive responses, rather than in literary forms, written response is frequently perceived as a comprehension response, promoting an efferent, rather than aesthetic, reading of the text.

Articulated response (i.e., protocol analysis) researchers come from a variety of backgrounds and provide a range of interesting possibilities for the teacher. While I. A. Richards investigated "errors" (e.g., stock responses, presuppositions, sentimentality, etc.) in interpretation of a text, David Bleich, at the other end of the spectrum, developed a subjectivist theory of reading using similar techniques (Bleich, 1978). Richards was interested in critical judgment of poetry, Bleich in affective and associative response to literature.

With regard to method, Richards argues that the response protocols are a means for communication (a claim he also makes for literary criticism in general), and therefore need to be set out in essay form as a means for refining communication (p. 10). Bleich tells us he prefers the "essay form of the response statement mainly because of my success with it in the classroom situations that I face," though he claims it also provides the best means for examining the affective and associative responses of readers (1978, p. 166; p. 146). In both instances the researcher has drawn his conclusions based on evidence from the reader's articulated responses to a text.

Richards's "practical criticism" requires the teacher to encourage response to a text so the teacher may assist the reader in becoming a more sophisticated interpreter of the text. In one sense, Richards's approach may be likened to the use of an "essay" question on a literature examination or a prewriting activity for a traditional literary essay. In an earlier book on subjective criticism, *Reading and Feelings* (Bleich, 1975), Bleich reports the use of "reading logs" as one way to record responses. In addition, Bleich engaged his students in various activities such as asking students to select "the most important element in the story" and then examine their criteria for making the judgment (Bleich, 1975, p. 101). Both researchers' methods require response following the reading of the entire literary work.

Various other response researchers have invoked articulated response as a means for investigating the inner cognitive, affective, or psychoanalytic workings of the reader's mind. The tendency in this type of research is to analyze the response as "insight into the mental and emotional workings of readers" (Petrosky, p. 78). Researchers taking this perspective on the question of reader response remind us that we cannot assume invariant mental features for readers which determine responses to a text, and that adolescent readers are developmentally different from adult readers.

Some researchers perceive protocol analysis itself as a means for improving response. From the psychoanalytic end of the field, researchers are concerned with the subconscious determinants of reader response; Norman Holland's work is the best known of psychoanalytic approaches to response research (Holland, 1990). From the perspective of classroom research, Patrick Dias views the development of the ability to respond as a matter of responding through the use of protocols over time (Dias, 1987). He uses spoken protocols, articulated while the students are reading poems, in an attempt to record response as close to initial aesthetic responses as possible.

One protocol analysis study that attempted to follow Rosenblatt's insight that aesthetic response takes place during the actual reading of the text is James Squire's *The Responses of Adolescents while Reading Four Short Stories* (Squire, 1964). Squire sought to analyze the spoken responses produced during the reading of a story. Accordingly, readers were stopped at various points in their reading and asked for open-ended responses. Squire found that readers produced different emphases in types of responses at various points in the narrative. Evaluative responses tended to increase dramatically during the last reading section of the stories, while self-involvement responses peaked early in the story. But overall, the highest percentage of responses, twice as large as the other categories, were interpretational responses. Interpretational responses also rose in frequency at the end of the story, along with the increase in evaluative responses (p. 32).

Alan Purves, along with Victoria Rippere, also researched the types of responses adolescents provided in their responses to literature, finally settling on numerous categories characterizing a wide range of student responses (Purves with Rippere, 1968). The elements are grouped under four general headings: (1) Engagement-Involvement, (2) Perception, (3) Interpretation, and (4) Evaluation, and the elements represent common features of articulated response, e.g., moral reaction to characters or incidents, allusion, inferred irony, and affective evaluation, respectively. There is also a category for miscellaneous response, extraneous to the text, such as digression. The usefulness of the Purves and Rippere categories is that they provide a frame for content analysis of written protocols.

Purves contends that the elements he has derived are neither taxonomical nor exhaustive; he claims they are simply descriptive. And as James Squire points out in the preface to the Purves study:

> The elements of writing about literature are not necessarily identical with the elements of response. Reactions secured through written protocols may reflect more what students have been taught to think and feel about literature, rather than what they actually think and feel. (pp. v–vi)

All of the research using protocol analysis, whether it focuses on cognitive matters or affective matters, seeks to promote the articulation of response for communication or revelation. Readers must articulate their thoughts and beliefs, as well as exhibit their judgments, in protocol analysis research.

Poetic Discourse Response

On the other hand, one key mode of representing response to litera-ture—writing literary texts in response to literary texts—has not generally been explored in the research. Response through literary forms is represented in classroom technique, e.g., Kenneth Koch's work with children writing poetry. Recently, pedagogical possibilities in this area have been reported by contributors to an Anglo-Australian collection entitled *Readers, Texts, Teachers* (Corcoran & Evans, 1987, allusion to Rosenblatt's title intended).

In one sense, it is shocking how little attention has been paid to discourse conventions used in responding to literature, especially to how those conventions might affect the nature of the literary response. Richard Beach investigated the types of discourse conventions used by readers in responding to literature and found that written responses foster more interpretative responses, while taped oral formats foster more engagement/autobiographical responses (Beach, 1973). With the exception of Arthur Applebee's use of James Britton's concept of spectator-role discourse for protocol analysis (Applebee, 1978), little consideration has been given to the social situation and the discourse form of the response until recently.

Britton and his colleagues' research on functional writing, and Britton's theory of language development, are both useful for under-standing the value of aesthetic response and the value of responding in literary forms (Britton, 1970; Britton, Burgess, Martin, McLeod & Rosen, 1975). Britton et al. examined the school writing of large numbers of students and produced a theoretical system structurally similar to Rosenblatt's efferent and aesthetic reading model. They also attempted to account for the psychological role of the language user, another concern parallel to Rosenblatt's. Britton's functional model of writing describes three categories of discourse: (1) Expressive, (2) Transactional (not to be confused with Rosenblatt's transactional model), and (3) Poetic.

The categories are generally framed by concerns for audience and purpose. *Expressive writing's* audience is the writer herself, and it functions primarily as a means of generating and recording thought, though the category includes personal narrative aimed at a peer or a trusted adult. Expressive writing is frequently what those researchers investigating the internal nature of literary response receive when they ask for "personal" responses to literature.

Transactional discourse is writing whose purpose is communicating directly to an audience. The writer assumes the psychological role of "participant" in transactional writing, addressing the audience to communicate something or to accomplish a task. Transactional writing includes school essays, letter writing, generalized narrative, and other workhorse categories we teach. Transactional writing is what protocol analysis research often finds in interpretative student responses, especially if the student perceives his role as communicating his response to the literature to someone else.

The third category, *poetic discourse*, is what some teachers call "creative writing" (though all writing is creative, and we sometimes accept expressive discourse as a substitute for poetic discourse). Poetic discourse is less concerned with the efficiency of communicating to an audience or accomplishing a task, and is more concerned with the "shaping of a verbal object." Rather than acting as a participant in the linguistic communication, the writer of poetic discourse assumes the psychological role of "spectator," presenting a reflection on experience or a picture of that experience. The spectator role assumes language use for its own sake, and "not for any ulterior end, any purpose that lies outside the activity itself" (Britton, 1976, p. 30).

No such thing as purely transactional or purely poetic writing exists. Imagine that the categories occupy a continuum, with different types of discourse arranged along the continuum. The telegram would be at the extreme transactional pole and the imagistic poem would be at the extreme poetic pole. It is also helpful to visualize the continuum as parallel with Rosenblatt's efferent–aesthetic continuum, though not identical to it (Rosenblatt, 1985, p. 102).

Most reader-response studies use expressive or transactional writing for response protocols. Unfortunately, because it assumes a communication to an audience, transactional writing as a means for response can foster an efferent reading stance. Asked to present in writing or speech the "main idea" of a story, a reader is unlikely to assume an aesthetic stance to accomplish the task.

Transactional language can be used for aesthetic-response studies, but its use requires a translation of the initial aesthetic response by the reader. The teacher or researcher must then translate the response back into an aesthetic response when reading the protocol. To investigate aesthetic reading and response, as Rosenblatt suggests, the assigned task must focus on the "lived-through" experience of the text.

Expressive discourse presents greater opportunities for promoting aesthetic response because it is concerned with personal response, that which is closest to inner and initial cognitive and emotive response. Expressive discourse need not directly account for or even acknowledge the text in the reading transaction, and is favored by the subjectivist researchers for this very reason. Bleich, concerned with the hidden dimensions of psychological response to literature, encourages essentially expressive discourse in his research techniques.

In Applebee's review of reader-response research through 1977, he found that transactional writing was the key mode used for framing responses (Applebee, 1977). But he also argues that there is nothing limiting about responding to poetic discourse in transactional discourse. He may be right, but in the classroom, protocol analysis is frequently confused with comprehension instruction, so the form of the response is critical for aesthetic reading. In addition, the possibility for aesthetic response through transactional writing responses appears more likely if students learn to respond aesthetically through poetic discourse first. Even expressive discourse probably represents a better opportunity for eliciting aesthetic response than does transactional discourse.

Research in this category is most fully explored by Arthur Applebee in *The Child's Concept of Story* (Applebee, 1978). Applebee drew on the basic research of James Britton and his colleagues at the University of London Institute of Education regarding the functions of language, recognizing a need to consider the form of discourse expected in the response. Britton's sociopsycholinguistic theories provided him with a view of language to account for the development of literary understanding (Applebee, 1985).

Applebee's own research pays more attention to poetic discourse in examining readers' (ages two through seventeen) conceptions of story (Applebee, 1978). He argues that the concept of story possessed by the reader is based on learned behavior, i.e., learning aesthetic response is a socially learned behavior. Like Vygotsky and Rosenblatt, Applebee suggests the crucial role of form in language experience. Unlike other response theorists, he makes an important argument for examining poetic, i.e., spectator-role, discourse as a means for fully analyzing response, though he also uses transactional writing in his research as well (p. 16).

Applebee acknowledges that much of the task in analyzing response protocols is necessarily an attempt to "look through" transactional language to unveil the poetic response (pp. 16–17). He uses transactional responses as the primary data for his analysis, though he does make use of poetic discourse through the retelling of stories.

Applebee's point concerning response form and the acceptability of transactional response is well-taken. But aesthetic response is frequently short-circuited by students in the classroom, or ignored by the teacher, when transactional prose is used for recording response. Students do not understand the mechanism by which one makes the transition from reading poetic discourse to responding in transactional discourse, or they attempt a shortcut by reading the poetic discourse efferently.

Research recently conducted at the Center for the Learning and Teaching of Literature, of which Applebee is director, suggests that regardless of the final form of the response, poetic discourse plays a role in response. Judith Langer's recent studies, conducted at the CLTL, promote the cognitive concept of "envisionment" as a necessary first step in response, a term certainly related to the notion of spectator-role language functions (Langer, 1990).

Probably the only way to assure an initial aesthetic stance is to require students to respond in poetic discourse. Responding in poetic discourse presents no teacher expectation for efferent reading to the students, nor does it allow the student to initially avoid the poetic response by writing the transactional response first.

Imagic Response

Implicit in the notion of the spectator role assumed in producing poetic discourse is the cognitive concept of imagery. Researchers specifically studying imagery's role in reader response have documented the sustained imagery production which is activated during reading. Using think-along procedures and postreading interviews, Long, Winograd, and Bridge discovered that not only did students report imagery (personification, metaphor, onomatopoeia, etc.) at points in the reading expected to elicit such response, but also at stops not expected to do so (Long, Winograd & Bridge, 1989). They also noted that in the absence of instructions to do so, students nevertheless reported imagery when reading both expository and literary texts. Such findings prompted the conclusion that imagery pervades the thinking process and that image construction may be a key part of the process of reading.

Paivio's dual code theory of comprehension also identifies imagery as related to cognition (Paivio, 1986). The theory contends that, in addition to a linguistic and verbal system, our cognition includes a nonverbal imagery system. Though interconnected, these systems are independent of one another. Expounding upon the importance of imagery aroused by text material, Paivio suggests that wording asso-

ciated with dominant imagery can sustain and attenuate a general imagery context which is thus continuously or repeatedly evoked as the text is read. He hypothesizes that "the overall theme might be represented partly by a relatively specific image that recurs in some form throughout the text to recurrent cue" (p. 227).

One way to understand what Paivio is saying in this regard is to consider the recurring images in *The Great Gatsby*. The ephemeral and isolated existence of Gatsby is not merely established by initial comparisons and contexts that describe Gatsby when first seen by Nick ("silhouette of a moving cat," arms "stretched out toward the dark water," etc.). In addition, it is reinforced by a myriad settings, behaviors, conversations, and descriptions that suggest Gatsby's vulnerability, his disappointment, his estrangement. Gatsby's vision of deathless Louisville nights spent with Daisy is but one "recurrent cue" which carries us to the crescendo of Nick's connection of Gatsby with the early Dutch sailors (not "settlers") seeing for the first time the beauty of "the fresh, green breast of the new world." And many previous images have established and enriched Fitzgerald's final description of us all as beating on, "boats against the current, borne back ceaselessly into the past." The concreteness and the mystical qualities of this metaphor, its physical and frenetic implications, its elation and deflation, make sense in light of the web of imagery which has preceded it and now plays an essential part in our evocation of the text.

The *Gatsby* example may also help to exemplify what Alan Purves considers the role of imagery in contributing to "central tendencies" in reader response. Purves theorizes that "at a general level" images are common and that the pattern of images and emotions found in a work contribute to a "central imagic and emotional meaning" which constrains the idiosyncratic images of the reader and subordinates them to a total pattern established by the text (quoted in Sadoski, Goetz & Kangiser, 1988). We envision these patterns as an "imagic umbrella."

Recognition of the importance of Purves's theory is emerging. For example, analyzing the pattern of images reported by college students in response to three popular short stories of similar structure, Sadoski et al. specifically cite the existence of such a central imagic current while noting that the structure of the story máy affect this flow (Sadoski, Goetz & Kangiser, 1988).

At this point it is appropriate to introduce a note of caution and overall emphasis regarding imagery and its role in reader response. We do not want to suggest, as some reading researchers appear to, that language concerns are not the primary consideration in the reading

act. First, the mental images are evoked by language, and second, the articulation of nonlinguistic processing is done through language. Language-based teaching is essential in English classrooms.

Researchers have also begun to turn their attention to illuminating the relationships between imagery and other dimensions of reader response. In the study already cited, Sadoski also examined the relationships between imagery, affect (emotional response of the reader), and structural importance (the significance the reader gives to the event or incident in terms of its importance to the design of the whole story). He concludes that imagery and affect may be "inherently related." For example, strong affective reactions produced imagery whether or not students attributed importance to the section of the text which elicited the response. He also found that the degree to which affective responses influenced reader's perception of importance was influenced by imagery. Applying these findings in the classroom will show that image making and elaboration are far more than mnemonic devices.

What may be most important for our purposes, however, are the research findings that one important function of imagery may be to increase the degree of involvement, interest, and enjoyment of reading (Long, et al., 1989; Nell, 1988). Concentrating upon the vividness of a reader's imagery, defined in terms of its strength and clarity, Long concludes that such vividness is a predictor of aesthetic response. The "active" reader generates imagery which will in itself help promote more engagement with the text during reading. In this regard, imagery is not only to be seen as a functionary helping carry the burden of "processing" the text, but a part of the aesthetic response and a means of sustaining reading pleasure.

Unarticulated Response

In addition to articulated response studies, there is a second type of research into literary response, which seeks to evaluate response before it is articulated. Research on unarticulated response, sometimes called "passive ability" research, does not rely on readers' written or spoken responses or re-creations of the text, but attempts "to try to go beyond such descriptions and statements and try to get closer to the response itself" (Hansson, 1985, p. 213, 217). This research tradition actually antedates the articulated research paradigm defined by I. A. Richards's study, originating with Alan Abbott and M. R. Trabue's 1921 study of poetic judgment.

"Passive ability" as a cognitive concept is related to the idea of tacit knowledge, or "knowing more than we can say." Passive ability, however, should not be confused with the notion of a "passive" reader. Hansson's use of the term is best seen in a discussion of his conclusions from a major study of unarticulated response:

> The *passive* ability of the less-educated readers to notice and judge linguistic, literary, and experiential qualities were much more developed than their *active* ability to verbalize their interpretations and experiences in written statements. (1985, p. 217, emphasis in the original)

In other words, in an articulated response (protocol analysis) study these readers might appear less sophisticated because they are unable to fully articulate their responses.

The importance of unarticulated response in the aesthetic transaction is best illustrated through an anecdote told by the scholar, essayist, and poet Guy Davenport in his collection of essays, *Every Force Evolves a Form* (Davenport, 1987). Various well-regarded friends of Davenport were proclaiming the virtues of Charles Olsen's poem, "The Kingfishers," one going so far as to call it *"the* modern masterpiece" (p. 95).

When Davenport set out to teach the poem in a graduate course, he reports "there was an enormous amount of text that would need looking up" in order to teach the poem (p. 95). Even after he began teaching the poem in class, he found much about it that was inexplicable. He and the students in the course became so obsessed with understanding the allusions in the poem that one of the students even drove from Kentucky to Gloucester, Massachusetts, to confront the poet himself concerning several intriguing, but hopelessly obscure, references. Even that interview failed to fully "explain" the poem.

Finally, faced with an invitation to contribute a scholarly study of Olsen after the poet's death, Davenport turned for help to the friends who had first praised the poem. In speaking at length with each of the champions of "The Kingfishers," Davenport found that "none of the admirers of the poem had the least notion as to the meaning of any of the allusions, obscure or otherwise." And, though one of his friends had "recited 'The Kingfishers' with passion in my living room . . . he had no more understanding of the poem than my cat" (p. 97). These readers of the poem, sophisticated adult artists and intellectuals that they were, were filled with unarticulative feelings and thoughts.

Unarticulated response, as a research topic and a teaching approach, has had its share of influential scholarly supporters over the years, including two important British contributors to the seminal 1966

Dartmouth Anglo-American English Teaching Conference. In his contribution to a collection of reports from the literature study group at that conference, entitled *Response to Literature,* James Britton observed that "A sense of literary form . . . may become articulate finding expression in comment and criticism, but equally it may not; and this, as pedants, we find very difficult to admit" (Squire, 1968, p. 5).

In the same volume, the psychologist D. W. Harding directly addressed the problematic nature of articulated response as a teaching and research technique: ". . . overt response (verbal, etc.) may indicate very little of the inner response" (p. 11). Even so, unarticulated aesthetic response has received much less attention than articulated response in research and in the classroom over the years.

The obvious classroom problem with unarticulated response is that the teacher needs some evidence of response and a useful form of response for class discussion and evaluation. Indeed, the research methods used in unarticulated response studies do provide some useful techniques for framing responses. These techniques also provide a means for students to respond when they might otherwise remain inarticulate. Furthermore, the unarticulated response techniques provide an initial response from which articulated responses can develop.

Unarticulated response research uses various methods, many of which can be used as teaching strategies. Gunnar Hansson charted responses on a semantic differential scale; Alan Purves asked participants to choose critical questions they would prefer to answer about a text; and Allan Abbott and M. R. Trabue asked subjects to choose the *best* and *worst* versions among four versions of the same poem (one of them the original text, three of them altered versions).

Abbott and Trabue rewrote poems by altering rhyme (unrhyming the poems), meter (disturbing the rhythm), and tone (making one version more "sentimental"). Readers ranging from grade 5 through graduate school selected what they judged to be the *best* and *worst* versions from among the four versions. Students in elementary and high schools and those in the first two years of college showed a tendency toward selecting the sentimental version as *best.* Readers in the last two years of college and graduate school were more likely to choose the original version as *best.*

Abbott and Trabue used "essential characteristics" as their criteria for altering the poems; Anderson, in a reworking of that study, used "poetic convention" for altering the texts (Anderson, 1988; 1990). Teachers using the technique in the classroom may use any appropriate and useful criteria relevant to the needs of the lesson and the student.

Purves, in the International Association for the Evaluation of Educational Achievement study, asked ten-year-olds, fourteen-year-olds, and those in the final pre-university year in fifteen countries to choose the five questions they thought the most important to ask about William Carlos Williams's "The Use of Force" from a list of twenty provided (Purves, et al., 1981, pp. 153–154). Questions ranged from "Is there a lesson to be learned from 'The Use of Force'?" to "Does the story succeed in getting me involved in the situation?" to "Is this a proper subject for a story?" to "What kinds of metaphors, images, or other writers' devices are used in 'The Use of Force'?"

He repeated the procedure with additional stories, investigating the types of questions the readers chose (p. 89). He found "that each text is unique not simply in its meaning and emotion but in the critical perspective that it elicited from students, and this across a broad spectrum of cultures and educational systems" (Purves, 1979, p. 810). In other words, one poem elicited primarily analytical responses, while another elicited primarily personal responses. The text had a constraining influence on the reader response.

On the other hand, Purves also found that some readers chose the same type of questions regardless of the text they were reading, thus exhibiting a personal response pattern. Purves goes on to suggest that this "whole web of connectedness and dispersion needs to be the province of research in response to literature" (Purves, 1985, p. 68). The combination of personal response patterns and text-constrained patterns appears to empirically support Rosenblatt's theories.

Gunnar Hansson's literary response research used verbal scales based on semantic differentials to provoke response. Hansson's research method asked readers to respond to poems on bipolar scales using, among others, these descriptors: *tragic–happy, bitter–sweet, simple–complex,* and *vibrant–static* (Hansson, 1973). Other research conducted in this area has used single pole scales, e.g., "0 1 2 3 4 5 6 7 Happy" (Hansson, 1985). The semantic differential technique was developed by psychologists to account for differences among individuals in ability to verbalize thoughts and feelings (Osgood, et al., 1957).

Hansson required readers to respond every two lines in the process of reading an extremely difficult twelve-line poem, using twenty-five different verbal scales. He also required them to respond to all twenty-five scales at the end of the poem. The readers represented three different levels of sophistication: "experts (scholars and teachers of literature), university students studying literature, and skilled workers with only seven years of compulsory school in their childhood" (Hansson, 1985, p. 217). The results showed a remarkable similarity in response profiles on the verbal scales.

What is important about Hansson's study is the demonstration that less-educated readers still have similar aesthetic responses to those of the more educated readers. The difference between the less educated and the better educated lies in the ability to articulate the response. In addition, his research would seem to indicate that the starting point for consensus in a group of readers lies in the initial aesthetic response rather than in literal comprehension of the basic plot and character.

Unarticulated response research's most intriguing finding, supported by Hansson and Purves's research, is this idea of a "central tendency" in response to a particular text:

> Using the semantic differential with a variety of readers from all walks of life, [Hansson] showed that there was a central tendency in the response to a poem. Only when the readers began to articulate their responses did diversity enter, for then readers began to focus on different aspects of the poem, began to make critical statements. (Purves, 1979, p. 809)

While the associative responses and even the interpretative responses may differ more than they resemble each other in the classroom, the aesthetic responses should show a general similarity in unarticulated response. The verbal text appears to influence, or constrain, the aesthetic response of the reader.

In other research, after having high school students read a short story by Jessamyn West, Golden and Guthrie used a forced-choice methodology to explore reader response in terms of reader background beliefs, reader empathy, text events, and text conflict (Golden & Guthrie, 1986). Discovering that readers defined the conflict in the story according to the character the readers empathized with most, they suggested that plot perception is related to such affective dispositions.

Using semantic differential scales made up of the readers' own responses, as well as personal interviews, Miall found considerable agreement among college students asked to interpret elements of a Coleridge poem, thereby suggesting that "a number of invariant features in the text were determining their response" (Miall, 1985). The personal interviews revealed individual differences in readings of the poem, concerning mainly personal experiences and attitudes.

Literature in the Classroom

Purves says that most responses are "schooled" responses, so the community influence on initial aesthetic judgment may be critical. Abbott and Trabue's study discovered a similar "central tendency" with regard to student evaluative judgment in response to altered versions of poems. The consensus response we ask of our students is there at the beginning of their responses to a work of literature; discussion of the work adds diversity rather than commonality to response. Commonality after discussion of a text can come only from a centralized authority or developed consensus.

Purves's review of the research seems to demonstrate the points that Rosenblatt makes about the necessary constituents of the aesthetic transaction being the reader and the text in a social context. The text does constrain response; the central tendency in response demonstrates that fact. On the other hand, there are individual responses to a text, responses that become more individual the more they are elaborated.

In Purves's words, "the twin ideas of central tendency and dispersion are important to a theory of response and to research in response" (Purves, 1985, p. 64). As he suggests, a student may respond analytically to one literary work, and evaluatively to another, but in both cases may focus on characters. Also, most of our students might respond to a central incident in a short story, though they might respond in different categories or forms. Opportunities for response must include opportunities for individual response, while the teacher must look for the commonalities of response.

The need to evoke an aesthetic response without translating it into a communication to others through transactional writing, but still providing a means for expressing the response, is served by unarticulated response, whatever the mechanism for responding. Semantic differentials do constrain the response, but they also allow the teacher to set the parameters of response or the focus of the response based on basic judgments about the work. Rewriting and comparing versions of a poem allow the student to make holistic judgments without recourse to articulating a rationale.

Whether response is articulated or unarticulated, the essential fact is that response must account for aesthetic experience with literature. The two best approaches to that necessity appear to be approaches that avoid all possibilities of efferent response, namely unarticulated response and articulated response through poetic discourse.

These approaches do not account for all types of reader response, nor even all types of literary aims and instruction. They may simply be what Purves calls "mediating exercises," a crucial step on the path to a fully articulated response (Purves, 1990). But this mediating activity enhances, maybe even allows, the aesthetic response, a necessary response expected from the reader of literature.

Indeed, there is room, and probably a need for, efferent reading in the English class, but there is already too much of that in the curriculum as it is. Transactional writing about literature is a necessity, but if used exclusively, we believe students will see the task of reading literature as primarily efferent in nature. Transactional writing assignments that do not first attend to the aesthetic response of students are doomed to efferent activities as well. Without aesthetic reading there is no literature study; there is only the inappropriate use of literary texts.

2 Practice

PART I: UNARTICULATED RESPONSE

The activities which follow in part I require aesthetic reading and response on the part of students, though the initial response to the text does not rely on articulating a response in speaking or writing. Students are provided with alternative means for responding to a text, and each activity illustrates an attempt to get as close to an initial aesthetic reading and response as possible. Congruent with Rosenblatt's theories, use of these activities and instruments will focus the "selective attention" of the student on aesthetic reading and provide a means for response accessible to students of every ability level.

The teacher determines the form and nature of the response by designing the instrument for evoking response. However, aesthetic linguistic experience is the focus of each of the following activities: all responses are based on students' direct reading of language, not on reiterating the teacher's authoritative reading. The teacher's responsibility is to provide classroom situations where aesthetic reading is encouraged and an aesthetic response is the expected response.

Designing and developing instruments for inviting unarticulated aesthetic response does take planning time, but really no more time than developing efferent comprehension questions. In addition, developing many of the instruments and activities requires the teacher to engage in aesthetic reading, thereby focusing explicitly on aesthetic and linguistic issues prior to comprehension and interpretation concerns. The aesthetic response is not taken for granted or neglected as a classroom expectation.

Altering Text

One basic method for emphasizing aesthetic response to literature provides students with more than one version of a literary text for comparison. Two or more versions of a literary work, one the original version, with other versions rewritten by the teacher, furnish an

27

opportunity for students to respond without articulating critical reactions.

After reading the different versions of the literary text, students may be asked to pick the *best* version, the *worst* version, the *funniest* version, the *oldest* (either text or author) version, the *most sincere* version, etc. Students may even rank the versions, based on any criteria the teacher, or the students, select.

Normally, students must make critical judgments about a work of literature in isolation from other texts. The use of rewritten versions of a text in comparison to the original provides for concrete choices. For example, given the following versions of the Emily Dickinson poem "We Never Know How High," students were asked to select the *best* and *worst* versions to see how poetic conventions affected evaluative response.

We Never Know How High

Version 1:

> We never know how high up we are
>   Until we are called upon to arise;
> And then if we are true to the plan,
>   Our statures can touch the skies.
>
> The heroism that we recite
>   Would be an ongoing thing,
> If we did not the cubits warp
>   Because of our fear of being kings.

Version 2:

> We never know how high we are
>   Till we are called to rise;
> And then if we are true to the plan,
>   Our statures touch the skies.
>
> The heroism we recite
>   Would be a daily thing,
> Did not ourselves the cubits warp
>   For fear to be a king.

Version 3:

> We never know how high we are
>   Till we are told "Rise up";
> And then if we are true to the plan
>   Our statures touch the skies.
>
> The noble deeds we recite
>   Would be a daily thing,
> If we did not the cubits warp
>   For fear to be our best.

Version 4:

>We never know how high we are
>>Until we're told to rise
>And then if we fulfill the plan
>>Our heights can reach the skies.
>
>The noble deeds we recite
>>Would be a routine thing,
>If we did not the measures warp,
>>Afraid of being kings.

Version 2 is the original poem, the meter has been disrupted in the first, the rhyme has been removed in the third version, and in the fourth version, less poetic diction has been substituted for the original. Student responders tended to choose the altered rhyme and meter as worst, and the original and altered diction as best (Anderson, 1990). They were asked for evaluative critical judgment in this case; they could have been asked for personal response ("Which one do you like the best?").

Different criteria for altering text should be used to evoke other types of responses. In their 1921 classic study, Abbott and Trabue rewrote poems using the criteria of rhyme, meter, and, reflecting one of the major critical concerns of their time, "sentimental" tone. Rewriting parts of a short story in another style, or implanting text from one author into another's text, also provides altered texts for comparison and response. Providing versions of a text altered by the teacher has the added benefit of assisting the teacher in recognizing aesthetic elements in the original.

Although rewriting the text is generally the teacher's responsibility, differing versions of various literary works already exist. For example, the original published version of Bryant's "Thanatopsis" from 1817 omits the first seventeen lines and the last fifteen lines of the version published in his 1821 *Poems*, the one we read today. The additional lines substantially change the poem. For teaching *Hamlet*, the 1603 "bad quarto" contains an especially hideous rendition of the "To be or not to be" soliloquy. The most ambitious students might compare the recently published variant unfinished manuscripts of Twain's "The Mysterious Stranger" with the one most of us have read, edited and completed by A. B. Paine in 1916.

Whether the teacher rewrites the text or finds variant texts, the technique requires the teacher to provide the criteria for comparing the texts. For instance, students may be asked to choose the more "mature" version of "Thanatopsis." After students make the initial choices, the discussion that follows invokes the criteria the students used in determining "maturity" (e.g., length of poem, ambiguity of theme, quality of diction) in the versions of the poems.

Responses to gender differences can be explored by changing pronouns and names in a poem from one gender to the other (e.g., Susan Cory, rather than Richard Cory) and asking students to decide which of the two versions of the poem is better. In the follow-up, we have found that student response to a beautiful and rich woman's suicide is frequently quite different from their response to a man's suicide. Switching authors' names on Elizabeth Barrett and Robert Browning love poems, and asking which is more *male* or more *female* in tone and sentiment, can also be quite revealing of student assumptions concerning gender and literature.

Altered text can be used for unarticulated response as an end in itself, since some students will not be able to articulate a rationale for their choices. On the other hand, most students can point to the literary work under consideration with examples of what they mean, even if they cannot express it in formal terms. Reasons for the relatively consistent negative responses to the unrhymed version of "We Never Know How High" range from "It doesn't feel right" to "The meter has been altered." In both cases students have made the same aesthetic choice, while their articulation of personal criteria for judgment differs only in degree.

The research reporting a "central tendency" in response to a text is based on unarticulated response research (including the verbal scales research, which will be discussed shortly). Given a common means for response, and a method that discounts ability to articulate a response as an initial criterion for response, teachers will find much more community in response than if they rely on free, articulated responses. Individual patterns of response will appear, but the responses generally begin by recognizing aesthetic features of the text.

Verbal Scales

Unarticulated student response can also be captured through the use of verbal scales. Given Britton and Harding's warnings that articulated response may reveal little of the inner response, and that much research in literary response only measures differences in ability to respond, verbal scales can provide equal opportunity for all students to respond. Verbal scales generally use a "semantic differential" as a yardstick for response.

Verbal scales are generally of two types: (1) bipolar, with the two poles defined by opposing adjectives and usually having approximately seven points between them (e.g., Bright 1 2 3 4 5 6 7 Dark); and (2) unipolar scales, defined by a single adjective and numbered beginning with zero (e.g., 0 1 2 3 4 5 Strong). The bipolar scale allows a choice of degree in assigning value to a semantic choice. The unipolar scale, with its "0," allows the respondent to reject the category entirely as inappropriate to the situation or text as well as to rate the degree of response.

The choice to use "Hot–Lukewarm–Cold" or "Happy 1 2 3 4 5 Sad" or "0 1 2 3 4 5 6 7 Honest" is up to the individual teacher, but the choices must represent related semantic categories and the students must understand what the scale represents. More than one scale may be used for most literary texts, with each scale attending to a different aspect of the work. Students may also mark the rating scales at different stages in the text to record patterns of response during the reading of the work and to chart any changes in their responses over time. In fact, verbal scales marked more than once during a reading often show structural or emotive "movement" during a poem, story, or play.

One example of this phenomenon can be seen by using the technique with the Edwin Arlington Robinson poem "Richard Cory." Readers rank the central character after each stanza on a unipolar "admiration" scale as well as a bipolar "like–dislike" scale to chart their personal responses to the actions and circumstance of the character. The "turn" at the end of the poem is more obvious to students when they chart their personal responses stanza by stanza.

> Whenever Richard Cory went down town,
> We people on the pavement looked at him:
> He was a gentleman from sole to crown,
> Clean favored, and imperially slim.

How do you feel toward Richard Cory?

> Like   1 2 3 4 5   Dislike
> Admire 0 1 2 3 4 5 6 7 8 9 10

> And he was always quietly arrayed,
> And he was always human when he talked;
> But still he fluttered pulses when he said,
> "Good morning," and he glittered when he walked.

> Like   1 2 3 4 5   Dislike
> Admire 0 1 2 3 4 5 6 7 8 9 10

> And he was rich—yes, richer than a king—
> And admirably schooled in every grace:
> In fine, we thought that he was everything

To make us wish that we were in his place.

Like   1   2   3   4   5   Dislike
Admire   0   1   2   3   4   5   6   7   8   9   10

So on we worked, and waited for the light,
And went without the meat, and cursed the bread;
And Richard Cory, one calm summer night,
Went home and put a bullet through his head.

Like   1   2   3   4   5   Dislike
Admire   0   1   2   3   4   5   6   7   8   9   10

What can be intriguing in this exercise is that, whether a student begins by liking or disliking Cory, after the final stanza the response tends to shift significantly from the earlier "like–dislike" ratings and to move dramatically up or down the admiration scale. The technique need not be restricted to personal response; students could just as easily have been asked, "How does the poet (or speaker or narrator) feel toward Richard Cory?" to produce similar movement on the scales.

Verbal scales need not be restricted to short poems. Charting Hamlet's psychological state on a scale of "insane–sane" at the end of each act of the play mimics the intentions of the "Richard Cory" exercise. The use of verbal scales for response to *Hamlet* allows students to express their opinions during reading and permits them to return to their previous responses to analyze the changes in their responses during the reading of the play.

Using verbal scales during the reading of a literary work is one of the better ways to chart aesthetic response, especially given Rosenblatt's definition of aesthetic reading as being concerned primarily with response during the reading of text. Hansson's research showing central tendencies in response across widely differing populations used repeated verbal scales during the reading of literary works.

Charting student responses to the actions of literary characters represents only the most obvious way of using verbal scales. The complexities of "style" and "tone" may also be addressed using verbal scales. In fact, Hansson contends that verbal scales are particularly well-suited for exploring stylistic and structural qualities of literary works (Hansson, 1985, p. 228). For instance, consider the very complex instructional problem of tone, especially in a book such as *The Adventures of Huckleberry Finn,* and the way the use of a verbal scale permits response:

The author's tone in the [fill in the specific episode at the appropriate point in the book] episode in *Huckleberry Finn* is:

	Somewhat Serious			Somewhat Comic			
Serious	1	2 3 4	5 6		7	Comic

Because Twain is often simultaneously serious and comic (seriocomic or ironic), the verbal scale allows each student to express his or her view of how comic and/or serious Twain is being during a particular episode in the book.

This simple scale can be used throughout a reading of the text as a way of comparing specific scenes and establishing a baseline for comparison and judgment. The symbolic geography of Huck Finn's journey can be developed using a "civilized–uncivilized" semantic differential as a step in exploring key scenes and a key theme. Many other descriptors are certainly as useful as the one above, again depending on which criteria the teacher is interested in promoting in students' responses.

Traditional questions asked of literary works, such as questions concerning character development and conflict, can be transformed into verbal scales as a means for all students to provide an initial response, regardless of the importance or level of the question. The question, "Does Janie develop self-awareness and self-direction in *Their Eyes Were Watching God*?" can be transformed into verbal scales used at key points in the Zora Neale Hurston story:

> Who decides·what Janie will do at this point in the story? (If it was completely the choice of the other person, circle 1; if it was completely Janie's choice, circle 7. Circling 4 means you think it was equally Janie's and the other person's choice.)

> Other   1 2 3 4 5 6 7   Janie

The same question can be asked using a semantic differential:

> At this point in the narrative, is Janie an active participant in the decision making, or a passive follower of the wishes of others?

> Active   1 2 3 4 5 6 7   Passive

Either verbal scale requires the reader to situate Nanny, Joe, Tea Cake, the judge, and others relative to Janie's development as the author of her destiny. Using the verbal scale repeatedly (at each point that she marries, when she moves, in the flood scene, when she shoots Tea Cake, and in the courtroom scene, e.g.) demonstrates character growth in a method similar to the "Richard Cory" activity.

The verbal scale also allows for *degree* of responsibility to be assigned in each instance. Students then possess a means for describing Janie's autonomy in relation to the strong figures in her life while dealing with one of the novel's crucial critical debates. The articulation of their reasons for the response can follow, but each must first respond. Students can also see how they responded in the context of the other readers in class. Debates frequently arise out of differences in initial ratings, and students, having committed themselves to a public response, now find it necessary to defend and articulate that response. But in each case, the initial aesthetic response occurs before the translation necessary to communicating the response to another.

The scales also provoke responses that would not occur in free response settings. Unarticulated response does not mean unthinking response; it means that a mechanism is provided for the initial response prior to its articulation. The technique conforms to Rosenblatt's notion that the aesthetic response necessarily precedes articulated response, though it is not a free response.

There is certainly room in the curriculum for free response, if only by default, when we do not provide any guidelines for reading and response. In the above cases, however, the teacher structures the response possibilities. Thus reader response is not inhibited by teacher structuring; on the contrary, the readers' attention is directed toward aesthetic qualities they might not otherwise concentrate upon or even recognize.

Choosing Critical Questions

One method used in the 1973 IEA international assessment asked readers to choose from among a set of critical questions the ones they thought were the most important to ask about a particular text (Purves, et al., 1981). Patterns which surfaced in the types of questions students chose provide insights into student perceptions of the purposes of response. Purves found that different texts provoked different types of consistent responses, though many students did have preferred response patterns they favored, regardless of the nature of the literary work. Students also tended to choose questions they thought the teacher wished them to choose initially; Purves suggests that the consistency of individual response was tied to the students' perception that only one type of response was acceptable.

Alan Purves's "elements of response" categories, based on analyses of reader protocols, posits four main types of response: (1) Engagement-Involvement, (2) Perception, (3) Interpretation, and (4) Evaluation, and a fifth category for miscellaneous other responses. Questions using each of the above categories (in the same order for purposes of illustration) might look like this:

Which question do you think is the most important question to ask about [the work of literature in question]?

1. Has the incident in the story ever happened to you? *Involvement*
2. When was this story written, and who was the author? *perception*
3. Is the ending of this story ironic? *interp.*
4. What qualities make this story a good story? *-Eval.*
5. What would you rather be doing than reading this story? *(misc.)*

The above questions are only illustrative in a meager way. Purves's categories are broken down into many subsets, described in *Elements of Writing about a Literary Work: A Study of Response to Literature* (Purves, et al., 1968). The categories are descriptive, not hierarchical; no category is perceived as more difficult than any other. Indeed, the categories really measure response *preferences*, rather than ability to respond.

The results of choosing critical questions can be used to determine the type of literary investigation to which the students, or this particular work of literature, will be the most receptive. There is likely to be a central tendency in the questions chosen, determined partly by the work and partly by the literary and social interests of the class.

The question-asking activity can also be designed without reference to the Purves categories. Teachers need not ask a range of questions from the Purves categories, nor conform to any idea of comprehensiveness in the categories. Categories of questions provided to students might include literal comprehension questions (for them to choose, not to answer), inferential questions, structural questions, literary theory questions, poetic technique questions, historical and biographical questions, or personal preference questions.

In response to reading *Moby Dick*, students might choose among the following "large" questions the most appropriate question to ask in response to the completion of the novel:

Rank in order of importance these questions about *Moby Dick:*

1. How accurate is Melville's picture of whaling, and is he scientifically correct in his writing about whales?
2. Is Melville writing from an ethical or religious viewpoint?
3. Are the characters in *Moby Dick* representative figures?
4. How is Melville's novel similar to Hawthorne's *Scarlet Letter*?
5. Could this book have been shorter?

Choosing the questions is as useful an exercise in exploring students' literary values as answering them. Rank-ordering the above questions asks the student to reflect on the aesthetic experience of the text and the purpose in reading it. Discussions of student rationales for their question choices permits an examination of the nature of literature and reading; the activity raises aesthetic issues.

Using the above question-choosing activity guarantees an aesthetic response, whereas the question, "What is the theme of *Moby Dick*?" guarantees an efferent response. There is no way to answer the theme question without teaching students that there is a "theme" to *Moby Dick* they should have understood in class discussion or found somewhere in the text.

Literary Cloze Techniques

Teachers wishing to mix some "comprehension" instruction with aesthetic response to literature may provide students with a poem disassembled into an alphabetized list of words, a technique suggested by Ascher Rivlin (personal communication, February 18, 1988; see Rivlin, 1974, for a comprehensive program aimed at aesthetic approaches to poetry reading). The students create, or reconstruct, a poem from the list of words. The key here is that the students re-create the meaning in the poem, though they may not comprehend the original poem, or even come up with a different poem entirely.

Poems sound like poetry even if read as alphabetized lists of words. Below are the thirty-nine words of Tennyson's "The Eagle," presented in alphabetical order:

a	he	sun
and	he	the
azure	he	the
beneath	him	the
clasps	his	the
close	in	thunderbolt
crag	lands	to
crawls	like	walls
crooked	lonely	watches
falls	mountain	with
from	ringed	with
hands	sea	wrinkled
he	stands	world

Just from this list of words, anyone can see that this is a nature poem with exceptional alliteration. In reassembling the poem, the students construct meaning through language, but they also construct an aesthetic object. Another variation on this exercise is to jumble the lines and have the students re-create the poem, or create their own poem, by reordering the lines.

A variation on traditional cloze techniques can also be used to explore quite a few conventions of poetry, depending on what is left out of the poem. In the following activity, based on the W. B. Yeats poem "Death," the emphasis is on re-creating the meaning of the poem. Students are asked to fill in the blanks with the words on the right, words removed from the indicated places in the poem. (The correct words appear in brackets.):

Nor [dread] nor hope attend	(death)
A [dying] animal;	(dying)
A man awaits his [end]	(died)
Dreading and [hoping] all;	(hoping)
Many times he [died],	(dread)
Many times [rose] again.	(derision)
A great [man] in his pride	(breath)
Confronting [murderous] men	(man)
Casts [derision] upon	(rose)
Supersession of [breath];	(murderous)
He knows [death] to the bone—	(end)
Man has created [death].	(death)

In the above activity, the words removed from the lines have been retained for the reader's use. The deleted words need not be supplied for some exercises, or substituted words may appear in the text. As with the altered text activities, the substitute words may focus on a particular quality the teacher wishes to stress in reading a literary work.

Such cloze activities characterize the unarticulated response versions of what Peter Adams calls "dependent authorship," i.e., assuming the role of author in response to a work, which will be discussed in the following section (Adams, 1987). These unarticulated cloze activities are a useful way to initiate students into dependent authorship activities.

PART II: ARTICULATED RESPONSE IN POETIC DISCOURSE

These following activities focus primarily on responding· to literature in the form of spectator-role, or poetic, discourse. The instructional emphasis is on writing literary texts rather than expository texts in response to literature, i.e., using poetic discourse to respond to poetic discourse, rather than using transactional discourse to respond to poetic discourse.

It is certainly valid to write an expository text (transactional discourse) about a poem (poetic discourse), or a persuasive essay or descriptive report about a novel. But this common instructional situation means the student must first respond aesthetically to poetic discourse and then translate the response into transactional discourse. The expectation of a transactional response, without careful structuring, may predispose the student to take a shortcut by reading in an efferent manner, avoiding the path from poetic to transactional discourse.

Primacy of the initial aesthetic response is the first consideration in each of the following activities. Many current instructional situations require an initial efferent stance on the part of the reader, especially if the student is to write a critical response. Articulated response in poetic discourse attempts to maintain aesthetic reading and response by presenting a task in that particular mode of language. The following activities promote aesthetic reading by asking for response in aesthetic language and form.

Imagic Umbrellas

Many texts are structured by an intentional unfurling and juxtaposition of imagery. For example, in Bradbury's *Fahrenheit 451*, the teacher could draw the immediate attention of the student to the numerous analogies, metaphors, similes, etc., which make up the fabric of the author's portrayal. Indeed, it is not difficult to develop a string of "study guide" questions which will acknowledge the density and appropriateness of the imagery used in the initial twenty or so pages of the novel. Of course, to do so is to suggest to the student that such imagery is part of the information to be carried away from the text. In other words, the imagery then becomes part of an efferent stance toward the work.

That students are rarely asked what they envisioned—what images they saw during and recalled after reading the selection—and instead are returned immediately to the text to find and list, sends at least two implicit messages: (1) response to images is a response unrelated to the goal of a critical reading response, and (2) the network of images which students envision contains fanciful and personal decorations to the reading and not fundamental ingredients in the students' continual construction of meaning.

Each of the activities discussed in this section takes issue with such assumptions, for each recognizes that the production of imagery is a continuous and important part of the reader's construction of meaning.

Theorists and researchers investigating cognition in reading suggest that imagery may be part of a nonverbal system by which the reader experiences and comprehends the text. In addition to fulfilling such cognitive functions, imagery serves as a means to increase involvement in and enjoyment of the reading. As such, it is an aesthetic experience in itself intended to sustain reading pleasure.

A common methodology to many of the initial activities in this section—soliciting the imagery students envision—relies upon and confirms researchers' findings. The activities also are designed in response to various researchers' contention that the pattern of images and emotions found in a piece of literature forms a constraining "imagic umbrella" to which the idiosyncratic images of the reader are subordinated. As can be recognized in the examples produced in the first few activities, the operation of the imagic umbrella accounts for a common and central imagic and emotional current, or flow, to a work.

Rather than asking a series of questions regarding setting, plot, theme, etc., teachers can introduce a reading selection by asking the students to report the images they recall after having read the piece or even a portion of it. One advantage of beginning in this manner is that students are rarely intimidated by such a request. This type of nonthreatening and nonevaluative question allows them to respond immediately.

As in all activities, teacher discretion, clarity, and preparation will make a difference. The teacher may need to first explain what is meant by imagery. To preempt any confusion as to what is being asked, teachers might first introduce a very short reading selection (several paragraphs) from another work and ask students to list all the sights and sounds which the reading elicited.

The teacher generally must be persistent in stimulating students to unfurl the more general and vague images produced. The idea is to make the imagery reports as vivid as possible without forcing the students into what they perceive as meaningless conjecture. Since connection between vividness of imagery and reader interest is significant, such prompting has value in itself. In our experience, there have been occasions where students have later asked to read the rest of the selection.

The decision the teacher must make is to determine the point in the reading at which to ask for such recall. A few factors should be considered:

• Is the text difficult to understand, at least initially? If it is, imagery reports will only reveal confusion, and the time is probably better spent helping students figure out what is going on.

- Is the text especially rich with images in the very first "scene"? If it is, students will enjoy reporting their visualizations, and engagement with the text will be increased.

- What do the text features recommend? For example, images embedded in discourse-level features (analogies, metaphors, etc.) are more apt to be recalled. In addition, researchers in reader response have found that plot structures affect imagery. In climax-resolution structures and in climax-resolution-surprise structures, the greatest and most vivid imagery was reported at the climax.

- Who is the audience? It might be prudent to limit the focus at first, i.e., more reports at short text intervals are less taxing to those who are low visualizers.

- Does the author's method recommend the activity? For example, the beginning pages of the novel often concentrate upon establishing the images associated with the characters and the settings which have prominence throughout the novel.

The Method

Select the amount of text to be read and determine the stopping points, those points in the reading where students will be asked to stop their reading and to write down all the sights, sounds, smells they associate with the scene. The first stopping point should be after the reading of a small portion of the text, yet one that marks a transition in the setting or establishes some structural feature of the text.

After the first stopping point, review the images recalled and created by the students. Solicit as many as possible, remaining nonevaluative. Cue more production by prompts which encourage students to speculate, to focus upon one object or person, to be more precise in their reports, etc.

It makes sense to review the basic situations that are about to occur in the sections that will be read. A little background allows for a smoother transition into the reading and also makes clear to the students that you are not asking them to simply repeat or summarize the plot (a frequent response when students are first introduced to this method). Distinguishing general plot events from specific imagery should be done quickly but persistently. Students should be reminded that a particular number of images is not expected.

The following discussion, which cites responses from a group of twelfth graders, is an example of the method applied to *Fahrenheit 451*. The opening of Ray Bradbury's novel is very carefully constructed to introduce and develop imagery associated with characters and settings. In fact, the novel begins with three "scenes" which are distinguished as much by their imagery as they are by their action. The first scene is only six paragraphs long. Another reason Bradbury was chosen as an illustration is that his images are quite vivid, and are often made that much more memorable by metaphor and simile. Bradbury's novel, then, is perfect for introducing this method.

A brief summary of the three scenes might be in order to understand the student responses that follow. The opening of the novel describes Montag, the fireman protagonist, burning a pile of books. The scene ends with his dark and slightly crazed smile of contentment. Bradbury then describes Montag's trip home, during which he encounters Clarisse, a young girl whose gentle but inquisitive manner is the beginning of Montag's own insurrection against the tyranny of the "451 society." Montag proceeds home to his wife, Mildred, and to the artificiality of their high-tech interior world of comfort. When Montag enters, he discovers that Mildred has once again attempted suicide.

The three scenes can be introduced with simple prompts:

1. In the opening scene of the novel, the protagonist, Montag, is described doing his job—"a fireman who sets fires."

2. Next, Montag walks home and meets a young girl in the neighborhood.

3. "Montag returns to his home and to his wife Mildred. She is not well."

Reviewing the images recalled and created as part of each student's response after stopping at the first section reveals the diversity of the students' responses. Some students "saw" the first section in light of the imagery explicitly drawn in the text. Their reports included, for example, seeing Montag as a crazed conductor, the pages of the burning books as flapping pigeon wings, the color of the fire and the sky as red and orange, the smell of kerosene, and the helmet numbered 451.

Some reported additional imagery that represented elaboration of the explicit image. For instance, a student identified the specific music he heard; he saw the "conductor" conducting. Others went beyond the explicit as they concentrated upon associated sounds (the crackle of the burning paper, the roar of the fire, and the pop of the first moments of combustion). One particularly poetic example revealed one reader's use of sound to animate and dramatize the scene:

> I pictured a buzzing sound, perhaps the sound made by the igniter.
> Moans of pain or immense struggle, but not made by people there
> at the scene but by the books. Maybe the moans I envisioned
> were coming from the spirits of people of the past—people who
> either wrote or read the books that the exterminator figure was
> burning.

In the last line of this report, the student assumes a metacognitive
position, i.e., he tries to distance himself from his production and
discuss the source of his reactions.

Indeed, researchers have reported instances of unsolicited inclusion
of such metacognitions amid reports of imagery. An activity which is
obviously derived from these observations is to have students write,
discussing how they believe their imagery came about. Not all students
are enthusiastic about examining their own thought processes, but the
appeal of writing about self as creator is, for some, irresistible. What
follows is the response of the student when asked to explain how he
arrived at his images (quoted above):

> When I read the "the blood pounded in his head" that gave me
> an idea of a strong pulse beat in this guy's brain, some kind of
> disorder, psychiatric. Since this guy (Montag) is destroying (killing)
> books, for example, just the thought of him killing doesn't present
> me with a picture of him having [sic] and stabbing a person once.
> This vision of him having a disorder makes me see Montag
> stabbing furiously, time after time but in 451 instead of a knife
> it's a flame thrower and instead of a person, it's books but the
> books are just like people. These books definitely have some kind
> of spirit. When Bradbury wrote "books died," he said that the
> books have spirit but not in those words . . . a book's spirit can
> come from the persons that wrote the book or perhaps from the
> book's audience, the people who read it—even if they enjoyed it
> or not. The whole scene is alive—the house jumps, books are
> eaten. Out of all this, I can see struggle, I can hear moans of pain
> and agony because the life from these books is being stripped
> away from them. They're not just dying, it's like they are being
> tortured.

This explanation acknowledges the context of the imagery produced
and represents an example of Applebee's notion of "looking through"
transactional prose as a means for reporting poetic responses (as does
the previous example). It also exemplifies the use of imagery to match
information from the text to the prior knowledge the reader brings to
the text.

What are being produced are imaginative speculations through the
use of imagery. Reader responses also indicate that when explicit
imagery is withheld, readers will provide it. For example, the opening

of *Fahrenheit 451* does not provide any description of the house being burned, but the twelfth graders saw it (e.g., "huge, old, three stories," "porch in front," "wooden fence along one side of the property, against which the pages of the burnt books gather"). Authors, in fact, rely upon such response and may intentionally curtail or omit description to provoke response (Iser, 1978).

Teachers can capitalize upon such intentionality by periodically asking students to fill in such "missing" elements. The quickest and easiest way is to ask for such elaborations as part of an oral response to a class reading of the text section. However, the teacher might also want a more sustained and deliberate speculation that can be articulated through imagery. In any case, it is best to follow the author's lead, that is, follow the structure provided by the text and place the student within it.

For instance, in *Fahrenheit 451*, after Clarisse's conversation with Montag, she returns home. Bradbury gives little description of that home, so students are asked to fill in this missing element by describing her home as they see it. Specific prompts are always helpful: What furnishings are there? What lighting? What pictures on what walls? What sounds and smells? In your visualization of the house, what time of day is it and is its exterior bathed in moonlight, harsh sunlight, or not illuminated at all? What does the exterior look like? Where is Clarisse in this picture you've created?

In the process of composing this vision, students are using imagery to synthesize and present their understanding of Clarisse as revealed in her dialogue with Montag and as suggested by the imagery which has been used to describe her. In the next scene, Montag returns to his own house and, not surprisingly, Bradbury fully describes its interior. It may be that having described Clarisse's house and clothed it in the images they see as appropriate, the readers can now read more aesthetically the very purposeful and detailed description of Montag's house that follows. Bradbury's method reveals such a purpose, and the teacher's method respects it.

The imagery created as part of "less is more" speculation is intended to respect and strengthen the relationship between the rich suggestiveness of the text and the cognitive and affective percolations of the reader. Imagery reports may also help the student reveal connections between scenes and environments.

In the previous activity, students were encouraged to build their pool of associated images to one scene so that they may bring them forth to a subsequent scene. By concentrating upon presenting parallel scenes, teachers can encourage students to bring forth images from a prior related scene or context and use them to help reveal students' understanding of the subsequent scene or context.

Again, in a 451 assignment, students were asked to describe what they saw, heard, smelled, etc., after they had read a scene in which a woman immolates herself amid her books rather than allow the firemen to burn them. Students introduced images that were not explicitly mentioned in the scene but emerged as means of expressing and representing understandings of that scene.

Student Example

- woman is young, wears white
- has pale skin, loose-flowing dress
- plants in the room
- smell of kerosene and the smell of apricots
- crackling of fire eating pages
- words floating about the room
- flashing lights outside
- placid expression on face
- the conversation Montag had with Clarisse can be heard
- the smell of old books replaced by the smell of kerosene

This student has incorporated images associated with Clarisse (smell of apricot, pale face, e.g.) into what appears to be an "interpretation" of the scene. Images such as the green plants appear to be symbolic complements to the scene, yet they are no doubt also there in the form of one of the most persistent images in the book, the life and animation of the burning books. Some "central imagic" flow appears to be at work.

Teacher-directed follow-up activity asks the students to consider the source of the images and hypothesize what the production of these images might be suggesting. The students are not always aware of the connections they have drawn. For instance, the student just quoted was surprised to hear that some of her imagery was associated with Clarisse.

Yet it may be best to tread lightly. Translating all poetic productions into transactional communications is not only confusing for the student, but theoretically impossible. Resonating images do not reside in discrete packages to be unpacked by prose.

One of the basic premises of this book is that teachers need to provide students with a variety of ways to express their understandings.

This is not to say that the traditional questions need no longer be asked; instead, less traditional methods and forms need to be used to give students access to their understandings.

One approach teachers use to reassure themselves they are not compromising instructional goals in the methods they have developed is to first list the questions that they feel the student needs to address. It is sensible then for teachers contemplating these methods to do likewise. In fact, students can list the questions they think are important, as in the Purves question-selecting strategy. But, the idea is not to develop an activity per question. Rather, it is to recognize how the activity has addressed or transformed the question.

The following are very traditional questions that might be asked of students who have read the first chapter of *Fahrenheit 451:*

1. What is the function of the first scene of the chapter?
2. Contrast the imagery associated with Clarisse and Montag.
3. Why is Clarisse seen as a danger to society?
4. What is the structure of the first three scenes of the chapter?
5. Why is Montag confused?
6. In what ways are Clarisse and her family different?
7. What is the function of Clarisse in the novel?

The list is not exhaustive, yet it is representative. In addition to considering the relevance of any imagery activities to such questions, teachers should consider how these questions might be answered if a transactional response were offered. For example, question 5 could be approached with circumlocution ("He doesn't know what to think!"), with subterfuge ("He is beginning to doubt what he has been told"), with myopia ("He doesn't love his wife anymore").

A more promising approach might be to have students assume the role of Montag and review the experiences of this confusing day. They can describe a dream Montag might have had prior to going to bed that night. Tell the students to make the dream a running collection of sights, sounds, smells, with no commentary or narrative in between. In point of fact, Bradbury suggests such an assignment when he briefly has Montag describe such a dream prior to his proclamation that "I don't know anything anymore."

The following are student samples of Montag's dream:

- Running—something chasing, a soft light, Mildred (wife) clinging to his leg, people on other side of road playing, reading, walking;

the words "Are you happy?" written on all three television walls. . . .

- A flame, a book, an empty street, soft rain, street lights, sound of a pill bottle being knocked over, the lights of Clarisse's house blazing, the machine, humming, curtains in Clarisse's window, the voice of her uncle, Clarisse asking, "Are you happy?"
- A smile, fire burning by itself, a man with smile standing in front of a mound of burning books, the scent of apricots and strawberries, the scent of kerosene. . . .

The activities described so far are interventions at points in the reading. Especially with more difficult novels, it is advisable to concentrate upon such medial assignments to allow students a way to offer their understandings as they read and as means to provoke emerging understandings as they continue. It is also possible to elicit more global responses from students that are offered after the completion of the entire reading and prior to any class discussion.

James Squire, an advocate of the need to find ways to provoke aesthetic response to literature, has suggested that the first reading of a longer piece of literature be a quick one, unencumbered by ponderous analytical perspectives. The purpose is not to let the meaning-giving critical perspective dwarf the meaning-making pleasure of reading.

Methodologically, this can be accomplished by having students move from the spontaneous production of a rich pool of imagery that represents their responses to the entire book, to an exploration of the sources of these images, to the creation of an intentionally organized network of images that represents the meanings of the book as they see them. To help students do so, the following format is possible:

Creating a Pool of Images

Initial Instructions

Write down all the images that you associate with _____.
Think of your mind as some sort of box that contains the sights and sounds you have collected as you have read. Empty that box and write down its contents in the next few minutes.

Step 2

Have students reread their list and then ask them to add a minimum of five additional images.
Note: One way then to solicit a more extensive response is to first

give students a brief period to produce their first wave of images. Then they are asked to produce additional images. Many students, after being asked to produce this second generation of images, explain that they found themselves "piggy-backing" images or reviewing their automatically recalled images to discover their source or to add detail and specificity to them. Some reported that in their attempts to produce additional imagery they went to the final images in the selection. The teacher might suggest these methods to the students.

Step 3

Review with students what they have produced, making sure they are "unpacking" vague images and that they are not simply summarizing the plot. Be ready to give prompts—character names, settings, methods as listed in the step 2 note.

Exploring Image Production

Discuss the imagery the students have produced, encouraging them to make some sense as to why they might have generated these particular images. Possible questions:

- How do you think this image relates to this other one?
- You thought this image was important enough to be remembered. Do you see any particular significance in it?
- What images seem to be ones the class as a whole reported?

The teacher's job now is to give the student a context in which to bring the images together into a creation the student sees as representing the work's meaning. For specificity's sake, reference will be made to Fitzgerald's *The Great Gatsby*.

Providing a Context for Image Creation

Initial Instructions

Now that you have got a pool of images to work with, consider yourself to be the writer of a *Great Gatsby* video production. You have decided that you will first show Gatsby in his pool just before he is about to be killed. Your video will be a collection of rapid images that cross Gatsby's mind and will dissolve, one into the other. Use the images you have reported and/or additional ones to create this video. Consider what images will end the video.

Step 2

Following the creation of the video, students discuss what their video might suggest about the meaning of *The Great Gatsby*. Then they are told to "play around with" the video so as to recompose it through addition, deletion, juxtaposition, etc.

Student Examples Reported by Eleventh-Grade Class

- silk shirts
- black riding boots
- green light at end of harbor
- sidewalks white in moonlight
- Myer Wolfsheim's human molar cuff links
- huge eyes staring blindly
- "you can't live forever"
- dark blood in the dust
- glow of light surrounding a mansion
- uncut pages of a book
- ring of a telephone
- boat against a current
- aimlessly wandering partygoers
- Gatsby's silhouette
- Gatsby sitting alone in his car
- ashes
- Dan Cody's yacht

A Couple of Student "Videos"

> The sun shines brightly but as Gatsby drifts in the water, the sun changes into blind, huge eyes which stare over dust and ruins. They look downward and dark spots of blood seep onto the dust. Gatsby's tears mix with the blood and soon the world is covered in silver. Below his feet are sidewalks white with moonlight. Daisy appears by his side and smiles. She gently whispers something unintelligible and then hands Gatsby a rose. The rose becomes a bouquet which becomes a blanket of roses covering a black coffin. A hearse passes by. Nick appears and whispers something again unintelligible. The colors of the flowers blend together. Soft pastels. Shirts float about the room like petals on a spring day, Daisy's laugh, the ring of money and the harsh

sound of a telephone ringing. All turns black with the last sight being the black leather of Tom's riding boots.

After all is black, a voice asks, "Nick, old sport, what do you make of all that?"

Daisy appears in a white, flowing dress. The camera next moves to her green and bright shining eyes. Tom's black riding boots can be seen in them, as can Dan Cody's yacht. Then to the human molar cuff links on her blouse. It pulls back to reveal the huge eyes of T. J. Eckleburg. They do not move as a hearse covered with silk shirts and flowers passes by. Daisy turns. She is dressed in Gatsby's silk shirts and Tom's riding boots.

The preceding activities demonstrate that, after the reading of a piece of fiction, certain prominent images remain with the reader. Since these residual images can also be produced in response to a piece of nonfiction, they can provide the pathway for the students to return to that moment or situation in the text from which the image(s) were generated. The following method can be used when autobiographies or biographies are read.

Method Used for Biographies

After the reading selection, students recall any situation or moment in the text which, although it might not have been fully described, evoked from them a strong reaction.

- Students list any images they associate with the scene or event.

- Students are asked to "get involved" in the moment by attending to a character with whom they empathize. It is recommended that students "enter" the character through first-person or omniscient points of view and in some form present the character's experience.

An example of the method applied can be seen in the following samples of responses. Maya Angelou's autobiography *I Know Why the Caged Bird Sings* describes her "growing up black" in a small Arkansas town in the 1930s. Many students were particularly attracted to one scene in which Angelou discusses how the family must camouflage Uncle Willy from a possible Ku Klux Klan visit:

Uncle Willy gave me his rubber-tipped cane and bent down to get into the now-empty bin. It took forever before he lay down flat, and then we covered him with potatoes and onions, layer upon layer, like a casserole. Grandmother knelt praying in the darkened store.

One Student's Entry into the Scene

> Willie is now inside an unlikely tomb. He is shaking so violently
> that the onions are moving all around him, making loud crackling
> sounds as the skins crumble. The onions are alive, as if moving,
> crawling over him, causing him to shake even more. The onions
> don't cause his streaming tears.

Research findings that readers are constantly generating imagery,
even in response to expository text, is an invitation to consider activities
that capitalize upon that inclination. One way to do so is through
having students respond to prose selections by transforming the prose
into "poetry" and thereby producing a concentration upon the images
that reside in the prose.

The process is relatively simple. Students first write down a few of
the lines that produced strong imagery for them. They then transform
these sentences into poems. They may delete unnecessary words but
must include all images. The teacher might encourage the selection of
lines that contain a series of images, for such text encourages the
separation of discrete images. A student example from St. John de
Crèvecoeur's "What Is an American?" shows the process.

Selection

> There on a Sunday morning he sees a congregation of respectable
> farmers and their wives, all clad in neat homespun, well-mounted,
> or riding in their humble wagons.

Student Conversion

> There on a Sunday morning
> A congregation of
> Respectable farmers and their wives
> all clad in neat homespun
> well-mounted
> riding in their own humble wagon.

The original images may be used as a template to evoke images that
"exist" as implied contraries to the ones presented in the text.

In the student example below, the tone of the "re-vision" is consistent
with St. John de Crèvecoeur's essay, but the contraries have been
"updated" as one would expect and encourage. Also, as the following
student example shows, the use of parallelism aids the production of
contrasting imagery:

> Now on a Sunday morning
> A congregation of

> Respectable merchants and their mistresses
> all clad in wrinkled polyester
> well mounted upon cushioned seats
> riding in their exhaust spewing cars.

Students report that the production of this update is accomplished quickly. Of course, the general imagery, with its concentration upon the congregation's apparel, body position, and style of transportation, respectively, determines the focus of each line. In addition, the selection of imagery for the last two lines is mediated by the desire to be consistent with the satiric tone of the first concrete image.

More important, separation of each line allows for the student to consider the implications of each image. So often, students swallow the imagery whole, treating each successive image as a restatement of the previous image rather than as an extension of meaning produced by an interaction with the previous imagery.

Also, especially if the imagery is embedded in abstraction, it may be helpful to encourage students to develop associated but concrete imagery. This can be encouraged by separating the lines and providing a format as shown next. It is important to note that students must be allowed, if not encouraged, to delete any exposition that encumbers their visualization.

Selection

> We are a people of cultivators scattered over an immense territory, communicating with each other by means of good roads and navigable rivers, united by the silken bands of government, all respecting the laws, without dreading their power, because they are equitable. We are all animated with the spirit of an industry which is unfettered and unrestrained.

Conversion

> We are a people of cultivators
>   (student's response to above line)
> Scattered over an immense territory
>   (student's response to above line)
> united by silken bands of government
>   (student response)
> respecting the laws
>   (student response)
> animated with spirit of industry
>   (student response)
> unfettered and unrestrained
>   (student response)

Student "Updated" Example

> We are a people of solicitors
>   junk mail filling the mailbox
> Cramped within city boundaries
>   young children pressed against concrete
> split by iron prejudices
>   bottles flying above brotherhood rallies
> disregarding the law
>   Ollie North and the American flag
> dulled by contentment
>   adults watching Saturday morning cartoons
> fettered and restrained

It is also possible to let the reader's felt response lead the way by asking the reader what situations or events in the literature spurred strong reactions. Although such moments may not be climaxes embedded within the structure of the work, they nevertheless may generate a good deal of imagery made vivid by interest and emotive response.

First, ask the students to list any situations which, although not fully described by the text, are suggested by it. Next, they list any imagery which they associate with the situations. They may want to fashion the imagery into a fiction piece or leave it at that—a collection of images.

Numerous implied imagery situations occur in poetry of course. Dramatic monologues seem especially effective in soliciting reader response because they invite the reader to compose a portrait of the speaker based upon what and how he or she speaks. For example, in Browning's "My Last Duchess," what does the duke look like to the students? Or in "Gloriana Dying" by Samantha Egar, what does Elizabeth I look like?

Dorothy Parker's "The Choice" offers readers a chance to show in their imagery production whether they have captured the whimsy of the piece. In the poem, the speaker describes her suitors: one, a gentleman farmer type who would have provided a world of luxury and comfort to the speaker and the other a romantic troubadour "sudden, swift, and strong" whose lilting song carried the day. More concrete imagery is attributed to the rich suitor. As the following excerpt suggests, the imagery associated with the winsome suitor is intentionally far more impressionistic:

> He'd have given me rolling land,
>   Houses of marble, and billowing farms,
> Pearls, to trickle between my hands,
>   Smoldering rubies, to circle my arms.

You—you'd only a lilting song.
  Only a melody, happy and high,
You were sudden and swift and strong—
  Never a thought for another had I.

A context to encourage the students to introduce their imagery might be to ask them to describe a photo of each suitor carried in the speaker's wallet. Each photograph should place the suitor in the foreground of a scene appropriate to the setting in which the students see the suitor. As much as these pictures might reveal the readers' sympathies, the imagery which will reveal their attitudes toward the speaker and the tone of the poem will be evoked by having them describe the speaker herself.

Such an exercise provides a response far more satisfying than one which asks the students to determine the tone of the poem and support the choice. Looking at the questions which follow the poem in the anthology from which it was selected reveals that the poem has become a strange amalgam of information, morality-play fodder, and prognostication:

1. What were the woman's reasons for choosing as she did?

2. Do you think she would make the same decision if she could choose again?

3. If you had to make the choice Dorothy Parker describes, which would you choose—love or money?

There are always readings which do not tax the reading skills of our students but which are nevertheless beyond their grasp because these readings ask for a maturity and life perspective which is beyond students' years. Put another way, stories were not written with grade-leveled anthologies in mind. Oftentimes, we either dismiss these works as inappropriate or convince ourselves to teach them so that they will be appreciated at a later date. Of course, a third alternative is to treat them as moral treatises and hit the lecture circuit.

Transactional writing may be attempted, but it may be that other forms of response are not only easier to produce but are more authentic. The method to help the reader generate and express understanding begins with recall imagery and may be intensified by reading the portion of the text which contains the imagery which provides a template for subsequent text. The teacher then gives the student a context to compose through that imagery.

Consider Hemingway's "A Clean Well Lighted Place." The story's famous, concluding "Nada who art in Nada" interior monologue is a piece of nihilism lost on even the most precocious teenage psychoanalyst. However, the beautifully crafted initial scene of the story presents imagery which not only represents the interior condition of the protagonist but, in effect, can be carried forth to help the reader represent and construct his or her understanding of the piece.

Assignment

> Follow the man home to his apartment after his visit to the café.
> Describe that apartment and the old man as you see them, taking
> care to have your description represent what you think is his
> condition.

Student Responses to the Assignment

- The old man goes to his bedroom, not a thing is out of place, two soft, white lights in the room, the man sits on the edge of the bed illuminated by a moonbeam through the window opened half way, closet door shut, no pictures on the walls.
- Man settles on a balcony, looking at the sea hearing garbled sounds of waves, dim light from the kitchen inside, alone, heavy draperies except at the door to the balcony.
- The old man sits in a chair with a dim light in the corner. His apartment is neat, organized; outside is a slum, noisy, smelly. His windows and shades are closed.

Dependent Authorship

Another approach using poetic discourse as the primary form of written response is sometimes called "dependent authorship." Pieces are removed from a literary text, and students must supply their own replacements. In this scenario, the students use the given text as their starting point, and their creative response is within the structure established by the original author of the text. This situation is less intimidating for students who have had little opportunity to respond in poetic discourse.

The approach is recommended for use with prose, but it can be used judiciously with poetry. It also overlaps into the territory of unarticulated response, namely, literary cloze techniques. It may be that this is the best way to begin student authorship. Start by making a poem into a "cloze test" by removing individual words at various intervals.

But true dependent authorship involves much more complex response to literature than supplying missing words. Previously quoted, this reaction of a twelfth grader to the opening of Ray Bradbury's

Fahrenheit 451, reveals that, more than some passive, efficient processing operation, aesthetic reading is a reciprocal activity between reader and text:

> . . . makes me see Montag stabbing furiously, time after time, but in *Fahrenheit 451* instead of a knife, it's a flame thrower and instead of a person, it's books but the books are just like people. When Bradbury said "books died," he said that books have spirit but not in those words. A book's spirit can come from the persons who wrote the book or perhaps from the book's audience, the people who read it. The whole scene is alive—the house jumps, books are eaten. Out of this I can see struggle, I can hear moans of pain and agony because the life is being stripped away from them. They're not just dying. It's like they're being tortured.

The reader breathes life into and receives breath from the images, settings, and psychologies encountered. When Harold Rosen observes that within all stories are contained the ghosts of other stories, he is acknowledging this actively composing reader (Adams, 1987, p. 121). That such intimations created by the text, and perhaps implicit in its drama, remain stillborn is not a concession to, but a requirement for, a concentrated and satisfying composition. Nevertheless, these "stories" are part of the reader's experience of the text, glitterings that surround and are contained within the text. We wonder what absent characters are thinking; we overhear unarticulated conversations; we compose interior monologues and imagine the perceptions of characters; we produce sequels.

Teachers can capitalize upon these reader proclivities and invest them with the nondiscursive language of literature by having students assume the role of author and write from inside the world of the text. In *Readers, Texts, Teachers,* Peter Adams coins such writing "dependent authorship" and explains that the students' response in these instances is dependent upon the original, not only in that it requires the original piece in order to assume full significance, but more important, because it is a response both provoked and constrained by the rich resources of prior imaginative activity constructed in the text (Adams, 1987).

Adams emphasizes that one of the most valuable rationales for "imaginative entry into the life of the text in the role of author" is that it is a means "by which they [students] can discover and explore elements of their response to the work that they could not grasp or articulate in any other way" (p. 121). As can be imagined, the appropriateness and effectiveness of each of these writing opportunities are relevant to the reading selection and to the instruction. As always, the teacher must consider the reason for the writing and the placement of it within the discussion and response to the work. There are a few essential questions the teacher must consider:

- Is the writing to be an immediate opportunity solicited without prior class or individual discussion of the piece?
- Will these writings be used as a basis for class discussion to help further understanding and appreciation of the reading?
- Will it come prior to the writing of any other form of response?
- Will the writing format be assigned to the student, an intentional and appropriate means to have the student re-address, find a way to consider, or bring to focus?

Whatever the case, it is best at first that the entire class be introduced to the possible dependent authorship opportunities and to make that introduction stress that these writing opportunities arise from the reader's curiosities. This introduction should use a short story, one that invites many possible entries into the text (not all do, of course).

The first response students are asked to give is a listing of all the images that they associate with the story. The rationale for doing so is simply that such imagery suggests the significances each student perceives. The imagery selected may help the teacher to establish such activity as a part of a strategy which itself can help students to see their own productions as representing a form of understanding. Another reason to elicit imagery is that in some form or another it inevitably finds its way into the writing. When used again, the images take on a symbolic, as well as descriptive, purpose. In the process, the inclination to tell or explain is subordinated to the urge to create and represent.

Students are next asked to list and share the writing possibilities that lie within and around the text. Then they can choose one that most interests them. At this point, the students write.

To envision the operation of these steps, consider Stephen King's short story "The Last Rung of the Ladder." The story's central focus is an incident in which eight-year-old, pigtailed Katrina, blindly trusting her older brother Larry to save her, calmly takes a swan dive off a crumbling loft ladder into a pile of hay he has frantically gathered beneath her. Years pass. Larry moves on to become a successful corporate lawyer, complete with assistants and fine leather shoes. Katrina's path is one of divorce and prostitution. At the time Larry begins the narrative, he has just learned of her suicidal swan dive from the roof of an L.A. insurance company.

The climax of the short story reveals that a few weeks prior to her death, Katrina had sent Larry a desperate letter, one that was not delivered because Larry had failed to pass on his forwarding address following his own divorce. In the letter, Katrina tells Larry that she would have been better off if he had not saved her that day many years ago.

Activity:

Step 1: Students Generate Imagery

Student 1

> mice running out of the haystack
> Pa's calloused hands
> the letter and all the forwarding stickers attached
> the hay scattering in air
> the softness of the haystack
> the swan dive Kitty performed at the barn
> golden pigtails
> the crack of the ladder
> the sweet smell of manure
> the loose rung
> crossed off addresses
> Larry's expensive clothes
> Kitty's pale face staring down
> Kitty's flight into the hay

Student 2

> the girl's blond hair
> the hay stuck on the kids' clothing
> the pale face of Kitty
> the November light coming through cracks in the barn
> the thump as Kitty fell
> blue denim jeans
> crinkled, rough letter with crossed out addresses
> blond pigtails, no breasts
> swan dive from the barn and the building
> CALL GIRL SWAN DIVES headline
> Kitty's cry—Larry's cry
> the nails loosening on the top rung

Step 2: Students List the Writing Possibilities the Story Suggests

1. Larry returning to the barn years later.

2. The letters exchanged by Larry and Katrina over the years.

3. Larry discusses Katrina with her last landlady; he enters her room.

4. Katrina's diary is returned to Larry.

5. Katrina's dream before her death.
6. Katrina on the ledge just prior to her leap.
7. Larry's actions/thoughts simultaneous with Katrina's thoughts on the ledge.
8. Conversation between the dad and Larry on the plane after trip to L.A. for the funeral.
9. Larry's dream the night of Katrina's suicide.

Step 3: Students Write

A few clarifications/recommendations:

- The student writing is not treated as a piece of writing to be revised and polished.
- The teacher may include options, especially if they have in the past proven to be productive ones.
- The teacher should be on guard for writing options which might produce efferent responses. For example, dialogues between characters at the end of stories can become barely disguised moral commentary as a character tells another what was learned by the student. Predicting how the student might handle a writing option is not an easy task, however. One student contemplated having Larry become a family counselor responding to phone calls, an epilogue of sorts. The student did not select the option, but it would have been interesting to see how it was handled. It might not have become simply a lesson-learned presentation.
- Experience has shown that continuation scenes which are little more than answers to readers' questions are not particularly effective or appropriate to the author's intentions. The issue is then one of selection. A student providing an answer to the dilemma of "The Lady or the Tiger?" does not go far beyond an answer. Writing the occurrences after the narrator in "August Heat" completes his letter is not very fruitful. In fact, students may see such assignments as guess-what-really-happened questions or as invitations to overturn the text and create farcical or farfetched endings.

Student writing opportunities fall into general categories, each of which will be exemplified and discussed through reference to the specific writing possibilities listed earlier. "Writing within" opportunities are events and situations that may be alluded to in the text but are not developed (writing possibility #2 above). In addition, such writing may be elicited by situations implied by the text (writing possibilities #6, #8). Option 3 is a writing possibility that crosses both categories since Larry mentions that he talked with the landlady, yet no mention is made of his entry into her room.

"Writing Within" Experiences:

Student Sample: Katrina's Thoughts before Her Suicide

> Her head was swimming with memories, with the sweet smell of hay and manure. Maybe I'm not worth it, she thought. Maybe it's good that Larry has forgotten about me. Anyway, it was probably only an accident that he never told me that he was moving. Or maybe he's busy with his job. He always had me to worry about and I caused him so much pain! She thought of the muffled yell from outside after the barn accident that night. . . . "Thank God she's still alive!" . . . it was a hoarse yell always followed by the crack of the whip and a sharp but much softer cry of pain. She had been sitting in her bed, cringing at the sound of each crack.
>
> She inched her way along the structure on the insurance building's roof, looking down at the cars crawling on the street. They looked like little faces, little ovals, every one of them a duplicate of her brother's face. She could see the faces so clearly, and they all bore the same terrible, anxious look. A look which concentrated solely upon her, as though she were the center of the universe, full of love and pain.
>
> It was her turn to bear that pain. What a gentleman he was, what courage to bear all that anxiety, to watch for her and fear for her carelessness. He bore it all for me. He put hay down.
>
> The floors of the buildings across the street looked so familiar. They formed a ladder, each floor a rung on that ladder—all the way down to the street. She listened to her voice echoing above the madness of the city, becoming fully awake and aware for a moment and forcing the visions out of her head. My turn, she thought. He suffered so long for me, and I had nothing to give him but love and trust. Trust . . . her mind clouded again. The hay was something she could trust. It was such a long, beautiful, shocking drop . . . the thrill of it but she could trust it. The sweet smell of hay when she plummeted into its depths, shrieking, laughing.
>
> She was still inching gracefully around the structure . . . if she could only get to where she was over the hay.
>
> Then she leaped: a perfect swan dive. She was like a bird—a baby bird—so trusting, opening its mouth to good and bad alike. Her brother always put down hay.

Another general type of student writing involves suspensions or discontinuations of the narrative's time frame. "Time-lapse" writing takes the reader to a future or past moment to show the genesis or consequence of an unresolved conflict or of a decision made by a character. On occasion, such journeys may place the protagonists in new surroundings or they may be revisitations to places of great significance. Flashbacks are included in this category. Epilogues, too, are types of extensions, usually condensed symbolic enactments that function not to answer reader curiosities but to add significances to events and conditions described in the text. Writing possibility #1 above is an example of this type.

Student Example: Larry's Return to the Barn

> The barn, which had been a huge structure when I was a child, had seemed to have shrunk with age and moved closer to the house. I walked slowly toward the door and had to duck my head as I walked through. I peered up at the ceiling. No light was shining through. The ladder that my father and I had rebuilt looked as old as the one that had broken and for a brief moment I thought I saw Kitty on the ladder. I suddenly became possessed and climbed the ladder, each rung a quest. As I reached the top, I looked for the birds, but none were there. There were no sounds. I suddenly felt what Kitty must have felt and I thought I heard Kitty calling me to let go.
>
> As I was falling, I felt a calmness that I never had had when we used to jump. Whether the hay was there or not did not matter.

Revisitation scenes are often written when students sense some psychological disequilibrium either within the character or within themselves as readers. In this case, the student did not want to let go of the ramifications of Larry's experiencing the trauma. He has stripped the scene of much of the imagery that he reported after his initial reading. The effect is to produce a concentration upon his feeling of isolation. Part of the impact of the last line is its distinction of Larry's psychological state from Kitty's.

Because of certain enigmatic qualities, some stories are more solicitous of continuation than others. In these stories, the teacher should consider assigning a writing that will bring that enigma into high relief. Katherine Mansfield's "Sixpence" explores the self-loathing of a father who, after listening to the exhortations of his wife, whips his child, his "little man," for the first time. The small boy, described as "good as gold as a rule, sensitive, affectionate, obedient and marvelously sensible for his age" had succumbed to one of his "mad dog moments," the consequence of which was a broken plate and a mother fearful that her son might be beyond her control, without the discipline a good whipping would instill. His lips quivering, but his eyes dry, the boy accepts his punishment.

Immediately recognizing the folly of his brutish behavior, the father assures the boy that it will never happen again, that the best thing to do is to smile and forget it, "old boy." But Dicky lies perfectly still, saying nothing, even when the father, in a desperate attempt at penance, lays a new sixpence upon his pillow. The story ends with what is a most obvious invitation for dependent authorship writing: "... but could even that—could even a whole sixpence, blot out what had been?"

After generating images in response to the story, the students collectively suggested the following writing possibilities:

- a flashback to the father's childhood
- next day—the father and mother conversation
- Dicky as a father
- a scene with Mrs. Spears and model children (Mrs. Spears, a friend of the mother's and an advocate of corporal punishment)

Three of the four suggestions are "time-lapse" options. However, in this case, the students did not suggest the writing they were given. (Pick up the story as the father closes door to the little boy's room.)

Student Responses

#1

He picked up the sixpence, walked over to the window, opened it quietly and dropped it. "There," he thought, "Daddy hurt me and I'm mad."

Dicky got back in bed. Then he heard the crying.

He walked to the hallway. There was his father next to the bed, praying, asking the Lord to forgive him.

Dicky walked quietly back to his room. He looked out the window and saw the sixpence shining in the moonlight.

#2

Dicky sat up in his bed. He glanced around the room in search of his piggy bank. As Dicky focused upon the bright peach piggy, he thought to himself, "Maybe I should be more mischievous more often." He shrugged his shoulders and pulled his covers away from his small body to reveal his clenched fist.

> Dicky opened his hand and looked at the money. "Daddy feels bad he hit me, but if he gives me money for hitting me maybe I should be bad more often."

#3

> The next morning, Dicky gets up and goes to the window. The glistening due shines on the leaves of the tree. The tree is grand and the sun shoots beams of light through its branches onto Dicky's face.
>
> With a light toss, the coin is lost in the trees, smothered by the leaves. As the sun continues to rise, Dicky gets dressed. He is going to play in the grass.
>
> Dicky rolled over, grabbed the sixpence, and sat up on the bed. He thought a minute. Then he stood up and walked to the window. As he looked out, the big gum tree in the garden cast a shadow from the pale moonlight. He held the sixpence up to the moonlight to see it shine. Then he threw it out the window. The servant girl picked it up and Dicky replied, "Keep it."

These are the best of the writings; most were more disengaged and mechanical. As these examples show, however, asking students to write the scene revealing Dicky's reaction produced diverse reactions. Some saw him as a little Machiavel who would use his father's behavior to his own advantage. Others added a moralistic scenario in which Dicky repented. A few immediately shifted the attention back to the father's trauma (most likely in response to the question asked at the end of the story).

The story is enigmatic in this regard and, of course, the father's pain and the reasons for it may be the focus of the story. However, the great majority of the students were unsympathetic toward Dicky, and portrayals of his disaffection were rare. Discussion revealed the sources of that reaction. A boy defended his portrayal of Dicky as resilient, if not conniving, by referring to part of his description: "marvelously sensible for his age" (a description probably included to temper reactions that he is somehow deranged and to show the compulsion behind Dicky's periodic moments of Dionysian enthusiasm).

The situation can also provoke subjective responses, as when one girl proclaimed, "It's just that he's like my snotty spoiled sister. He needs discipline." In such instances, take students immediately back to the text of the story (in this case, the description of Dicky previously quoted) and have them thus review the context of the story. Indeed, such a return to the text seems an imperative, for unsympathetic portrayals of Dicky and miraculous recoveries run the risk of trivializing

the experience or making the suffering of the father ironic, thereby
eliminating from consideration one of the possible themes of the story:
unexamined capitulation.

Another possibility is to assign students an additional writing
assignment. Multiple writings on the same selection may be used as
a way to help students express additional understandings. In the case
of the Mansfield short story, the students were asked to compose a
poem Dicky might have written. Its title was to be "My Mad-Dog
Moments."

"Mad-Dog Moment" Student Examples

#1
Jack be nimble,
Jack be quick
but Jack is nothing
compared to Dick.

I ran away in the woods to play
and there I sat, while mother cried.

I was a dog, a wolf crying to the moon
Then a soldier hiding in a hole
and a sailor swimming in the sea.

I crawled stealthily to the window
where my true objective lay
So in I crept and then I leapt
and pounced on a little girl's tea.

In mom came, like a wild great dane
But, just like Jack, I knew my knack
And bounded away quite free.

#2
No book is ever touched.
No hangar out of place.
No crease ever unfolded.
No bed corners untucked.

The place is clean
whitewashed and such
not a speck of dust
Or a print of dirt.
except on those days when the room comes alive.

lions and tigers
running wildly through the wind
carrying chaos and adventure
wherever they may go

A voice yells from behind
but the lions and tigers keep running
'Til the voice dies out
and they are finally alone

#3
When that rumbling feeling
stirs inside, no one can
stop me
I run and play
and tantalize.
I would never hurt any one. It is just
my way of letting loose.
Like a lion out of a cage.
But I don't have rage.
I'm just being me, a little boy with
a mad-dog heart.

One student quite interestingly produced a piece which placed mad-dog moments in a new light, suggesting that the experience with the father will be so traumatic to Dicky as to change his imagination into a brooding and angry agent. The transposition of that anger into the inanimate objects of childhood offers another provocative moment for the reader:

The toy chest is filled with many toys.
At night, the playful beings came alive.
the soldiers marched back and forth.
The dogs and cats play chase.
All the dolls play house.
Everyone and everything is happy.
Oh?
A break in their happiness.
I see a teddy bear with tears trickling
    from his cheeks
No one asked him what was wrong.
Little teddy was left alone.

I am angry.
I want teddy to have fun like the rest.
I wish I was one of the toys
So I could play with teddy.

The point is not that these poems reveal a great deal more sympathy, sympathy that will provide a "correct" interpretation of the Mansfield piece. The point is that it makes great sense to next have students discuss how each of their writings relate. Inevitably, their reflection on the relationships between their reactions brings them back to the text and to a consideration and appreciation of their responses.

It may be that when the teacher assigns a few possible writing opportunities, the order of these activities may influence student understanding. This can be explained as a function of the writer's engagement in the writing, experiencing his or her "own" story. It is sometimes advisable that two assignments be given, allowing the student then to have the interplay between the two affect the construction of meaning. Experience in teaching the story will allow teachers to develop a rationale to help them decide whether more than one writing should be required, and which ones and in what order. The question of how much discussion should go on between and after these writings must also be resolved on a case-by-case basis.

Allowing students to write the dreams that characters might have had at strategic moments encourages them to bring their own intuitions to the surface. Dreams let students suspend constrictions of time and place, to juxtapose images, to escape from narrative cohesions, and to offer possibilities for consideration without committing to definitive interpretation. The dreams emerge as quite purposeful readings of the interior workings of the character's mind, and any enigmatic moments seem appropriate and subject to their own coherency. Their imaginative play is inevitably quite serious.

The following is a dream written in response to "The Last Rung on the Ladder." The guidance for this dream was not provided by the teacher but by the particulars of the writing assignment itself. That is, by designating that the dream is to be by Larry, and its occurrence to be simultaneous with Kitty's suicide, the student has provided herself with a method to bring the narrator's experience of a past incident (Kitty's fall from the ladder) to bear upon his re-creation of a parallel incident (her final moments before her suicidal leap). The crafting of the writing option is part of the composing act.

Student Example: Larry's Dream at the Time of Kitty's Suicide

It's Kitty's turn now. Kitty, as usual was dressed in her chequered shirt and faded jeans, her hair tied back in pigtails. Grasping the sides of the ladder with her hands, she cautiously persuaded her feet to move up the rickety rungs.

Up and up she went until she was walking up concrete stairs. Katrina now was upright, her hands by her side. A beautiful woman, tall and slim, with her cornsilk hair illuminated by a rift in the ceiling of the passageway.

Finally, she reached a door. In front of her was the beam, seventy feet above the barn door. She was on the roof of a building. She didn't look down as she steadied herself to a graceful position preparing to jump. She pushed off the building and as she did so, she opened her mouth to scream but at that moment she became a bird, a bright swallow with golden plumage, flying high above the earth without a care in the world. Just as she was safely behind the clouds, she began to skydive, twisting in agony, trying to gain control.

I tried to pile hay on the spot that I thought she was going to fall upon, but she kept drifting. I failed.

I ran to her . . . a torn cornstalk with its golden cornsilk spread all over the ground.

Not all dreams take on the narrative cohesion of the above sample. The *Great Gatsby* dream mentioned in the imagery section is a much more highly imagistic writing because students were directed to concentrate on describing a flow of images that might have crossed the character's mind. The guidance for the following dreams is slightly different. The teacher lists for the students some of the symbols that are used by the writer. No explanation of what they symbolize is offered or discussed. Students are directed to compose a dream that uses the symbols and is in the form of a narrative. Students are reminded that dreams are symbolic, often appearing to make no sense in terms of actual events that occur. Again, this operation can be seen in the following student dreams of Willy Loman the night prior to his suicide.

Student Examples

#1

Willy envisioned himself writing at a desk. It was hard to make out what he was writing, perhaps his will. As the picture became clearer he saw the light suddenly glisten off his pen—the inscription read "To Bill Oliver—the company's best." The scene faded. Now he saw himself standing in an open field. He was wearing a beautifully tailored suit. Soon the field started to sprout growth—apartment buildings! and offices! Willy noticed things were getting darker. He could see no sun, no moon, no stars. The only light was a small gleam that was getting closer and stronger. Linda emerged from the light carrying a candle and a pair of torn stockings. She gave him the candle and wrapped the stockings about his hands. Biff appeared out of nowhere and holding a key, unlocked the stockings that had by now become handcuffs. Willy was free and Biff was gone.

Willy was now in a car, driving very fast. He jammed on his brakes as soon as he saw it, but he hit it. Actually, he went through it, him. Willy jumped out from the car to see Ben standing there playing a flute. He stared at Willy, laughed, and then handed him a bag of carrot seeds. He winked. Willy was left alone.

#2

I dreamed I was walking down a quiet, dark street when I heard the shrill music of a flute. I put my hands to my ears but I could still hear the music. I looked upward but could see no speck of sky. The apartment buildings had grown even taller, so much taller! I heard footsteps behind me and turned quickly. It was Ben. He just looked at me, staring right into my eyes. Finally, he said, "William, the jungle has no place for you." He disappeared and I continued my walk. The music of the flute was lower now. I passed by a grocery store but there were no groceries for sale, only silk stockings. I went inside and Linda was there buying some. I screamed at her not to buy them that I would get her some. She paid for them and walked away without a reply. I looked up at the salesman and to my surprise, it was Biff. He was wearing an expensive suit and in its pocket was Oliver's pen. He looked up and said, "I told her, Pop—she has to buy her own stockings now."

#3

"You're well-liked Willy." The voice came from a woman, a woman he somehow knew. She wasn't Linda. The face faded and Happy's appeared. "I'm getting married today, Pop." The face becomes Linda's. "You're a success, Willy. Look all you've done for your boys." She sits quietly mending stockings, mending and mending. The more she mends, the more there are to mend.

Willy squirms and then he hears faint music that draws him to the window and away from Linda. Ben is standing in the garden. "William, you have to go out and accomplish something." Ben and the garden are closed out by the apartment buildings, growing taller as Ben has spoken. All the seedlings are swept away but one. Happy picks it up.

A final format for the dream is to have students present the character's dream solely in analogy. Especially when first being introduced to the activity, students should be provided with some analogies they might use. For example, when students studying *Macbeth* are asked to write Macbeth's or Lady Macbeth's diary entries as the play progresses, they are required to have the characters represent their condition by referring to some analogy.

To help them do so, a few analogies are listed, including Macbeth/ Lady Macbeth as trapeze artists, as children climbing a tree, as occupants of amusement park rides or as occupants in a car traveling on a modern highway (pardon the anachronisms). It is also helpful to identify for students the moments at which such dreams might be written (at the news of Lady Macbeth's death, the night after Banquo has been killed, before Lady Macbeth's suicide, at the news that Macbeth has been made Thane of Cawdor). The following student dream was produced after class discussion of the first two acts of the play.

Student Example: Lady Macbeth's Dream after the Killing of Duncan

> I had a dream that I was traveling in a Corvette with Macbeth. We were in the fast lane and exited from it rather than the right side. We went past three hitchhikers. One looked like me. Once we went off the exit, the entry ramp disappeared.

Kenneth Koch has shown that elementary school students can grasp the "poetic idea" or situation of a poem and write within the dramatic composition it uses. More specifically, the following activities recognize the student's ability to perceive the structural patterns and methods established within a poem. The secret to the activities is the selection of poems that are quite overt in the use of such methods. The following student poem was produced after the class was given a copy of Stephen Crane's "War Is Kind." The only preparation for the writing that followed was a simple cloze activity in which students predicted the wording of the third and fourth stanzas after having read the first two stanzas (see below).

War Is Kind

Do not weep, maiden, for war is kind.
Because your lover threw wild hands toward the sky
And the affrighted steed ran on alone,
Do not weep.
War is kind.
    Hoarse, booming drums of the regiment,
    Little souls who thirst for fight,
    These men were born to drill and die.
    The unexplained glory flies above them,
    Great is the battle-god, great, and his kingdom—
    A field where a thousand corpses lie.
Do not weep, babe, for war is kind.
Because your father tumbled in the yellow trenches,
Raged at his breast, gulped and died.
Do not weep.
War is kind.
    Swift blazing flag of the regiment,
    Eagle with crest of red and gold,
    These men were born to drill and die.
    Point for them the virtue of slaughter,
    Make plain to them the excellence of killing
    And a field where a thousand corpses lie.

Student Example

> Do not weep, worker, unemployment is kind.
> Because there is no paycheck coming in
> And the family will suffer,
> Do not weep.
> Unemployment is kind.
>   The flowing money between the hands of owners.
>   Children who have as much as they want.
>   These men were born to make big bucks.
>   A meeting room where a thousand associates bargain.
> Do not weep, boy, unemployment is kind.
> Because there is no green in your house,
> Rage at your pop for having no job.
> Do not weep.
> Unemployment is kind.
>   The crisp greenbacks in all the registers.
>   Made significant with the sign of Washington
>   These men were born to make big bucks.
>   Point for them the virtue of a business mind.
>   Make plain the excellence of money.
>   And a meeting room where a thousand associates bargain.

Another student work shows the range of student response to this format:

> Do not mourn, father, for cancer is kind.
> They say have hope and don't despair.
> Keep in mind the positive
> Do not mourn.
> Cancer is kind.
>   Infesting your body.
>   Day after day.
>   Your resistance wanes
>   Dragging you down and taking your hope.
> Do not mourn, mother, for cancer is kind.
> Your faith in God will pull you through
> Love for your husband will make him well.
> Do not mourn.
> Cancer is kind.
>   Hospital after hospital.
>   Bill after bill.
>   The hurt never stops.
>   The children's stares.
>   Dragging you down and taking your hope.
>
> I do not mourn for I must be strong.
> For this weary hollow-eyed figure before me.

Finally, students may write in response to their own initial productions, instead of in response to published poems. Of course, the basis for the writing may be drawn from literary works. For example, the following exercise has as its origin contrasts developed in Maya Angelou's *I Know Why the Caged Bird Sings* and Paul Lawrence Dunbar's "Sympathy." As will also be recognized from a review of the exercises, students' initial productions are observations, not intentionally composed metaphors. However, along the way in the dialectical movement from observation to the composing and selection of parallel descriptions, poetic creation emerges.

The procedure itself follows a few very basic steps. At first, all these steps are taken using the contributions of as many members of the class as possible and displaying the appropriate responses at each step.

Step 1: Present students with two contrary states or conditions. It is best at first to select subjects which evoke concrete images rather than abstractions.

Step 2: Students generate specific actions they attribute to the first condition or subject. Gather and "publish" the collective contributions of all the class members.

Step 3: Using these first-stanza images, each student is asked to produce one that represents the contrary state (the second stanza).

Step 4: Repeat the process with new contraries. This time all steps are to be accomplished by the individual.

A Few Class Contributions (Step 2) of "A Free Bird"/"A Caged Bird"

> A free bird
>> hops upon a branch
>> looks proudly down from the cliff
>> sings in the sunset
>> flies swiftly through open fields
>> hovers over the blue water

Student Example for Step 3

> A caged bird
>> jumps about from bar to swing to bar
>> pecks at its feathers
>> chirps too loudly under its cover
>> bangs its wings against the bars
>> sleeps in the dark

Students can compose each list in isolation and in no particular order. Have them select five images from each list and tell them to pair up descriptions which they feel "go together." They then may also rearrange the order in which the selected images are presented in the stanzas and add or delete any actions, making the pairings more satisfactory in their mind.

A related activity assigns students to first create a stanza of observations. This is followed by a final declarative statement which resolves the images. The writing of the second stanza keeps the original as intact as possible. It concludes with an antithesis to the first stanza's conclusion.

Student Example: Using "The Child"/"The Teenager"

> The child dances in the tall green whispering grass.
>   climbs over the soft sofa.
>   giggles at the circus clown,
>   chases after the bouncing ball.
>   plays with the empty box
> And she makes the most of what she's been given.
>
> The teenager walks through the grass.
>   slouches in the stiff chair
>   mutters at the clown
>   grabs the bouncing ball
>   avoids the empty box
> And she does not see what she's been given

Poetry as Response to Poetry and Prose

As mentioned previously, an excellent example of writing responses to poetic discourse through poetic discourse is Kenneth Koch's method described in *Rose, Where Did You Get That Red?* (Koch, 1990). Koch's approach to teaching poetry to children revolves around students writing a poem in response to a poem. Koch de-emphasizes literal comprehension of the text in favor of an understanding of the "poetry idea," or dramatic situation in the poem, which then serves as the impetus and the structure for student poems.

While Koch's method is quite popular, rarely do teachers ask students to compose poems as part of their response to prose readings. However, when the context for asking them to do so is within the realm of the text and its possibilities, the poems take on an appropriateness and comprehensiveness which may outstrip prose responses. In fact, often the poetry which is produced would serve nicely as a prologue or epilogue for the piece being read.

Yet the poetry is not assigned to have such a particular function; instead, as the example will show, it is introduced as part of a situational possibility in the text. Most of the time, the best "situation" for the poetry is as part of a character's representation of his or her condition.

Listed below is an example of an unguided response. Most poems can simply be assigned without the need for any prompt or format to guide the production. It is best to discourage rhyme because students often are unable to develop an appropriate tone when restrained by rhyme considerations.

Reading Activity

> Sherwood Anderson's "Lift Up Thine Eyes" is a short story which attacks the dehumanizing effect of mass production upon the workers. In the Bogel factory, the belt is God. Precision, cleanliness, and calculation are servants of the new religion of efficiency. On occasion, a worker becomes deranged, a victim of the stress.

Assignment

> Write a poem that might have fallen from the pocket of such a worker.
>
> *A student response:*
>   Always work accurately
>   Always work fast
>   Must develop a rhythm
>   Must never miss a beat
>   Don't think
>   Just work
>   Don't think
>   Don't wonder
>   Never be the snag in the line
>   Don't mess up while being watched
>   Don't mess up while not being watched
>   Never lose your ties to this reality
>   Never get tapped on the shoulder
>   And you too can work at Bogel.

This student was not provided with a model or given a recommended style, but it is obvious that she picked up on the staccato prose of Anderson as well as his incremental repetition. When the teacher selects prose readings which have such distinguishing features, poems are more readily produced.

No such overt textual influence is seen in the following three student poems, all based upon *The Glass Menagerie* by Tennessee Williams.

Reading Activity

> *The Glass Menagerie* by Tennessee Williams involves the struggles of Tom Wingfield, a young man asked to shoulder the burden of

supporting his fatherless family and, in the process, to give up his own dreams. It is revealed by a co-worker that Tom often writes poetry while working at the shoe factory.

Assignment

Create those poems that Tom "Shakespeare" Wingfield might have written on the back of match covers.

Three Student Responses

#1

Stamp, stamp, stamp
My picture is with my father's
and so is my soul.
We room together
while the presses forever roll.
Stamp, stamp, stamp.

#2

My ears ring from their persistence.
Pressure fills my head.
My body filled like a balloon stretched to its limit.
I search for a needle.

My life is filled with too much hay.
I journey, and work
My dream to find the needle
To burst my stretched shell.
Hay turn to green soft grass
A cushion I can finally enjoy.

#3

I fly my plane with just one engine
Avoiding enemy fire
I escape
I parachute across enemy lines
I am sailing on a boat hijacked by pirates
but escape.
I swim in a sea of sharks
but escape.
The movie's over, I am greeted with open arms
by jonquils and a hornless unicorn.

I will never escape.

Although each poem employs a different poetic technique, each reveals the empathy of the writer for Tom's "two-by-four" existence as provider for the Wingfield household. There is in all three a hint of the sardonic yet whimsical touch that rescues Tom from self-absorption. That the language of the poem intensifies rather than just preserves this voice of the character shows that students can write poems which are not simply paraphrased equivalents of transactional assignments.

Poem responses can also be guided by the teacher; in the following activities, the teacher provides some direction. This direction may be to provide a specific focus for the poem or a method to help in its production.

Teachers frequently ask students to describe the feelings and reactions of characters. One way to add depth to the response is to ask students to write a poem, the last line of which is given to them, in which the character presents his or her feelings at the moment. The last line is one taken from the text itself, either offered by the character as part of self-description or as an observation which has been offered by another character about that character. It is also possible to use an accurate and telling description of a character by another, but to transform it into self-description.

The best quotations to select are ones which suggest a change or transformation in the character. Below is the method applied to *Macbeth:*

Possible Last Lines

> "O, full of scorpions is my mind, my dear wife."
> (III, ii, 36)
> "I lack the season of all natures, sleep." (Lady
> Macbeth about Macbeth, III, iv, 40)
> "The time has been my senses would have cool'd
> to hear a night shriek." (V, iv, 10–11)

Giving Some Direction

Students are told they are to produce the lines of verse which might precede the selected quote. Before doing so, however, teacher and students discuss the contraries implied in the line of verse. The poem is to be two stanzas long. Each stanza is to be of equal length and is to reveal the previous and the present condition of the character, respectively.

Giving More Direction

Although some will neither need nor want more direction, most students will not be able to readily proceed without it. As in the above method, the assignment is explained to students, and the contraries implied in the statements are considered.

To help them explore these contraries, students are given a "once/ now" format perhaps similar to the one given below. Such a format is particularly appropriate in light of the many losses suffered by Macbeth. Teacher and class complete the first two lines so as to make clear what is expected and how the poem might progress.

Possible Format

> Once, the wind played among the branches of the trees.
> Now, _____
> Once, _____
> Now, _____
> Once, _____
> Now, _____
> Once, _____
> Now, _____
> "O, full of scorpions is my mind, dear wife."

A Variation

Response poems can also be encouraged by splicing and distributing a character's lines within the structure of a simple poetic format. Thus, Lady Macbeth's exhortation to Macbeth to "Look like th' innocent flower, but be the serpent under't," (I, v, 65–66) could be presented to the students as follows (student response included):

> Look like the innocent flower
> That blooms in the spring
> Beneath the invigorating sun
> In the Garden of Eden—
>
> But be the serpent under it
> Coiled for the strike
> Hiding in the shadows
> Avoiding the truthful light.

The above quotation is but one of many that contain appearance/reality contrasts. In fact, Macbeth is replete with lines that suggest or develop many contrasts, including fruition/decay, madness/sanity, light/darkness, among others. Teachers can compile a list of these lines and then decide how to place and distribute components of these lines within verse.

The preceding activity (once/now poem writing) is an example of requiring students to write within a provided form. Having already written within a given structure or format, students can now try to use that same format but within a different context.

Each of the activities offers the students such new contexts. Students use the structures provided, responding to what they have just written within that structure. In effect, they are responding to their own writing. The teacher's role is to look for situations in which such response is appropriate to help reveal additional understandings of the text.

One scenario looks like this: students have just written a "once/now" poem in response to a line of character description. The teacher realizes that a later line in the reading "updates" the condition described in the previously assigned line. Of course, since such continuity is to be expected as the author shows the progressive development or deterioration of the character, the teacher can choose and arrange the selected lines to help facilitate this understanding in the student.

Students copy down each of the "once" lines they have just produced. They are given another final line (which has clear relationship to the character condition implied or stated in the line they have been given) and are asked to complete the "now" lines. Below are student examples (including the first-response writing):

> Once the wind played among the branches of the tree.
> Now the tree has been uprooted by the violence of the storm.
> Once the song birds sang sweetly in the spring.
> Now only ravens cry in barren lands.
> Once grassy knolls and fields abound.
> Now only perilous cliffs and rocks exist.
> Once blue skies and sunshine were all about.
> Now storm clouds and darkness rule.
>
> "O, full of scorpions is my mind, my dear wife."

The student response to the previous response follows:

> Once the wind played among the branches of the trees.
> Now the tree is stripped bare of its leaves.
> Once song birds sang sweetly in spring.
> Now their songs have lost their harmony.
> Once grassy knolls and field abound.
> Now I see no beauty anywhere.
> Once blue skies and sunshine were all about.
> Now the day no longer enlightens me.
>
> "The time has been, my senses would have cool'd to hear a night shriek."

Because initial imagery must be examined to help make it appropriate to the new context given in the next final line, this exercise can be a challenging activity for students. For some students the recomposing will be too much, no matter how judicious the teacher is in the selection and guidance process. It is important to recognize the need to be intentional in the composition of the exercises, both in the selection of the final lines and in the construction of the first lines. Teachers must rely upon their own sensitivities to the text being studied. The previous example forces students to consider the movement of Macbeth's mind to its frantic and paranoid state.

Connecting this frame of mind to its perceptions of the external world is not poetic artifice for the sake of the activity, but is sensible in terms of the psychology of the character and the method of the playwright. The "cool'd senses" quotation is an extension of the motif, for now Macbeth is unable to use the register of his senses; his horrible interiority threatens to divorce him from natural instincts.

In the previous segment of this practice section, activities were described which asked students to bring forth a method recognized in a published poem and to apply it to another, more personal context. (A detailed explanation of the method was offered in the dependent authorship section, p. 54.) However, the following poem by a tenth-grade hockey player writing in response to a Walt Whitman poem reveals the impact of the method, and the italicizing in the text suggests the methodology.

When I Heard the Learn'd Astronomer

When I heard the learn'd astronomer.
When the proofs, the figures, were ranged in columns
    before me
When I was shown the charts and diagrams, to add,
    divide, and measure,
When I sitting heard the astronomer where he lectured
    with much applause in the lecture room
How soon unaccountable I became tired and sick,
Till rising and gliding out I wander'd off by myself,
In the mystical moist night air, and from time to time,
Look'd up in perfect silence at the stars.

Student Responses

When I open the book bag and drag out the books,
When I look at the meaningless words, phrases, problems,
When I try to think diligently, be imaginative, be a
student,
How tired and frustrated I become.
Till I slip away into the arena.
The sound of my skates plunging into the silk ice,
The smooth strides and the crackling echo,
And then the ease of the puck grabbing the net.

After gaining familiarity with writing in this manner within the easily recognizable structures of specific poems, students are asked to use that structure to write a poem that might be written by a character within the prose selection they are reading. For example, our hockey player's class might be asked to write a Tom Wingfield poem, the first line of which would begin, "When I . . . ." In effect, the form presented to the students would be the same as presented to them when they personalized the poem but, of course, they would now be writing within the persona of the character.

Applying the method to another work will make it that much clearer:

Reading Activity

"There Will Come Soft Rains" is a Ray Bradbury short story that satirizes humankind's blind dependence on technology. At the end of the story, nuclear war destroys the society, finally reducing to rubble the last standing edifice, a home replete with all the conveniences of the day.

Assignment

Students are to write a poem entitled "Technology Is Kind" to be found amid the destruction. They are to use Stephen Crane's "War Is Kind" as their model.

The Method

Prior to the reading, students read Crane's poem and write their own such poem using a topic provided to them ("Drugs Are Kind," "Sports Are Kind," "Love Is Kind," etc.). They then proceed to compose the poem assigned as a response to the story.

The sequence of the production is represented in the student example which follows. (The original Crane poem appeared in the dependent authorship section, p. 68.)

> Do not weep, student, for school is kind.
> Because your teacher threw failing grades
> And the affrighted parents scream at you alone,
> Do not weep.
> School is kind.
>   Systematically scratching pens on little notebooks.
>   Little souls who thirst for the "A."
>   These kids were born to work for the G.P.A.
>   The inexplicable teacher struts beside them.
>   Great is the college god, great, and his kingdom
>   A dorm where a thousand beer bellies lie.
> Do not weep, parent, for school is kind.
> Because your son tumbled in the neon classroom,

Scratched at his head, gulped and failed.
Do not weep.
School is kind.
　Swift typing keys of the computer.
　Thoughts processed but not digested.
　These kids were born to work for the G.P.A.
　Point for them the art of learning.
　Make plain the excellence of cramming
　And a dorm where a thousand beer bellies lie.

Here is an example of a student response to the short story using "Technology Is Kind":

Delight in your machines, for they are good.
Because they leave your mind soft
And life is once again simple,
Delight in your machines.
They are good.

Click, clock, shuffle, done.
Life is easy and good.
Men reclining.
Happiness throughout.
Press it, push it, all done.

Delight in your machines, for they are good
Because they give us the leisure we deserve
And we the worship they deserve,
Delight in your machines, for they are good.

Quick, swift, and efficient.
No one need sweat.
All is finished.
Feet up, hands crossed, and mind dead.
Press it, push it, all done.

People, delight in your machines.
All dependency is theirs.
Delight in your machines.
They are good.

Continuous dream diaries, or poetic diary entries, written within the persona of the character are also an effective format for incorporating the different methods of response discussed in this section. Dream diary writing can be an especially valuable and appropriate project for longer works, including novels. Such diaries are sustained pieces of writing which, in their continuous composition, involve constant reconstructions and presentations of meaning.

As the diverse range of poetic responses represented in this section are allowed to interact in the diary, students create a structure to continually transform their reactions and understandings of the text into more frankly poetic forms. This allows for a consistent movement from participant to spectator, an aesthetic movement which in itself provokes and represents different and new understandings. It also moves students away from plot recitation ("I have killed Macduff's family") and bare pop psychological explication ("I can't stand myself. I hate what I have done").

The diaries may be written after the reading of the entire text. Usually, however, it is best to have them "cover" a section of the reading. They are then collected and reviewed and returned. Before handing in their final diary entries, students are encouraged to review the entire diary and to add or delete or in any way edit it to represent their "final" understandings.

As in the other activities in this section, the teacher using diary writing must decide the degree of guidance to be offered the student. In deciding how to proceed in this regard, the teacher should keep in mind that the refinement of the individual responses is not the main goal; students will not produce perfect diaries or individual poems crafted through a series of revisions.

In most cases, students have already been introduced to some of the poetic response formats discussed in this book before they are assigned diary writing. However, it is entirely possible that the teacher may introduce the formats within the larger assignment of writing the diary. The teacher need only bring the response possibilities to one section of the text and review them with the class as they are produced.

No matter what the approach, the most important thing the teacher can do in helping the students to select and organize these responses is to indicate at what points in the story or play the writing should occur. The final goal is to let the students decide what type of writing is suggested by the text (a dream, a last-line poem, collection of images, etc.) at these points.

The following student writing is excerpted from a diary of Macbeth. The student was told at what points he should write. (Generally, it was designated that writing be done that reveals a response to the character's soliloquies.) The student was not told what format to use.

Act I, sc. iii (after first meeting with the witches):

Here I stand at the pinnacle
Why then am I torn?
Right is wrong; wrong is right.
Evil is good; good is evil.
Welcome news has thrown my life into unwelcome torrent.

Under a blood red sky, I ride into Duncan's castle. To
take from one so dear. The wind begins to howl.

Act I, sc. iv (after pronouncement that Malcolm will be the Prince of Cumberland):

My desire burns like a candle in my room.
The fever of power.
Should I grow weary of my own?
I hunger for a time of healing.
I must be aware that the earth moves under my mind's
landscape.

Act I, sc. vii (Macbeth's vacillation soliloquy; Lady Macbeth's exhortations to manhood; Macbeth's resolve to murder):

Will a murder set me free?
I see the sky burning rain.
He will die and live again, tonight.
Dislocated and suffocated, I grow weary of my own.
A day will come when an honest man
Will rule an honest age.
I must be gone on the rising tide.
Fulfill my destiny.

Act II, sc. ii (following the assassination):

Praying hand hold me down.
A dream: no stars in the black night. No sun in the
daylight. My corpse lies putrid, wizened, hoary. A rain
drenches the land for as far as one can see, but I remain
dry.

Act II, sc. iii (discovery of the deed):

The deed is not done!
I will travel across the fields of mourning forever.

Act III, sc. i (Banquo's soliloquy; Macbeth's meeting with the murderers of Banquo):

Banquo is to be feared and revered. My truths are not hidden from him. Once again the winds have begun to howl. I dream . . . I am talking to myself. There are two of me. One proclaims, "Once I vowed to submit my destiny to fate, but I have changed my mind. I killed Duncan deliberately, with premeditation. Chance did not crown me. Murder did. It fulfilled fate. Now I must assure that Banquo's son's fate is not realized. I must act." . . . My other self remains quiet. Then the two collapse into each other and wail in fear.

Act III, sc. ii (Macbeth's increasing paranoia concerning Banquo):

Damn the rest of the universe. I see my path!

Act III, sc. iv (Visitation by ghost of Banquo; plotting against Macduff):

Banquo in death knows all about me. A dream: The sun in the

sky makes me view my shadow stretching out to cover that sun.
I'm here in a palace of shame. In a cold lake of glass, I see my
reflection pass. I see the purple of the Lord's eyes contrasting the
scarlet of my lies. I walk through the valley of the shadow. But I
fear no evil. I have cursed thy rod and staff. They no longer
comfort me. I've conquered my past. I stand at the entrance to a
new world I can see. The ruins will soon have lost sight of me.

Act V, sc. viii (Macbeth's death):

My corpse dissolves and blows into the wind.
A driving rain cleanses the land.

Although only excerpts have been quoted, this wonderful piece of
writing is clearly a vision carefully crafted. The diary is built upon
images woven into a structure of their own. Some of the responses
are developed through some fairly extended dream descriptions. But,
essentially, there is a startling and effective economy to Macbeth's
proclamations. Also quite noticeable is the absence of plot summary.
The student steadfastly refuses to reduce this writing to a series of
barely disguised journalistic reports.

Equally important is that the student has been very responsive to
those images and sentiments presented in the play. For example, it is
quite obvious that the paradoxical language employed in the first aside
in Act I, scene ii, is incorporated into the first entry. Indeed, the student
has used the language of the play to compose his creations and to
build and organize the interrelationships between the entries.

Asked to create the dream that Macbeth might have had after
meeting with Lady Macbeth upon his return to Inverness, one young
woman wrote a diary response which even more concretely shows
the influence of the text upon students' productions:

> Tonight I had a dream that I was standing on a tightrope while
> plotting the murder of Duncan. Suddenly, the tightrope turned
> into a giant serpent. I looked down and viewed a pool of milk.
> From the sky, it began to rain—poisonous venom. I had to make
> a decision: to jump off the rope into the pool or to remain to be
> pelted by the evil venom. I began to tremble and I slipped off
> the rope. However, a hand reached out and pulled me up. It was
> my wife's hand. Together, we absorbed every drop of the poisonous
> venom.

It is doubtful that a transactional assignment could provoke such
insight. Most definitely none could provoke the poetic recasting of
dialogue which this scene represents.

In addition, the writing is not removed from its text; rather it has
fed upon the most basic resource of the text, its language. In fact, any

reader familiar with scene v, the very brief scene in which Lady Macbeth responds to Macbeth's letter and greets him as he arrives "under [her] battlements," will recognize the text. Macbeth is described as "too full of the milk of human kindness." Lady Macbeth prays to have her milk exchanged for gall and, as part of her plan to "pour [her] spirits" in his ear, she exhorts him to "look like th' innocent flower, but be the serpent under't." Not coincidentally, another student described Macbeth as seeing himself as suspended in a cage with bars of milk through which Lady Macbeth, dressed in white amid the darkness, attempts to chew.

Students will organize the diary in their own ways. No general prescription should be given. However, the first Macbeth diary to the contrary, the teacher can require the use of a few specific response methods to be repeated at designated points within the diary. The reason to do so is not to offhandedly give coherence to the student's product. Rather, as is consistent with the use of these methods as discussed in this section, it is to encourage poetic discourse and to provide the student with structure to help generate and fashion additional insights:

- Students are given specific last-line poems, each so distributed within the diary as to reveal the character's progressive development.

- Students are required to "update" a dream they have included elsewhere in the diary, at a point they feel is appropriate and revealing.

- At certain points designated by the teacher, students are to write a poem whose format the teacher also designates. This same format will reappear at strategic points, also designated by the teacher.

As much as it may appear that these scaffolding activities are imperative, the truth is that they may not be needed. Certainly, as has been mentioned, the diary excerpts quoted used no such direct methodologies. In fact, as has also been stated, the student was not compelled to write within any format. The teacher may decide to make requirements after reviewing the first "installment" of the diary.

It is also true that the use of any method is contingent upon the work to which it is being applied. For example, Gene Forrester, the narrator of John Knowles's *A Separate Peace*, undergoes a series of transformations as he confronts for the first time the primal nature and the "dark" in his heart. During the concluding chapters of the novel, he is saved from its threatening grasp and makes his separate peace.

For Knowles's novel, it would be sensible to require that students write a series of three "once/now" poems that would correspond with the periods of harmony, isolation, and enlightenment which are part of Gene's journey. The novel also offers the possibility of having the students juxtapose the possible diary entries of both Gene and Phineas. This dual diary method is especially enticing because the thoughts and reactions of Phineas are intentionally suppressed so that the reader can become immersed in the inferences of Gene's increasing paranoia or guilt.

Most of the time, dual diary methods include designated diary writings that ask students to consider the simultaneous reactions or perspectives of characters. A few of the required writings in *A Separate Peace* might include the following:

1. Phineas's description of the landscape below before he falls from the tree.
2. Phineas's description and reaction to the night at the beach.
3. Phineas's return to the tree following his return to campus.
4. Phineas's thoughts as he struggles to forgive Gene following the second fall, including a dream he might have had that night in the infirmary and his own "once/now" poem.
5. The dreams Phineas and Gene might have had the night Phineas died (following their reconciliation).

Nothing is written in stone here. The teacher may decide to have students write just a few excerpts from Phineas's diary, rather than anything exhaustive. The teacher may concentrate upon but one dual diary activity so as to juxtapose the single entries for purpose of discussion. Given the imprimatur that their nature and use is a function of the work and the teacher's objectives, the teacher might experiment with dual character diaries in *Macbeth* (Lady Macbeth/Macbeth; Macbeth/Banquo), *The Great Gatsby* (Nick/Gatsby; Tom/Gatsby), *The Scarlet Letter* (Hester/Dimmesdale).

PART III: A NOTE ON CURRICULUM AND INSTRUCTION

The activities presented here are not in any order necessarily, and there certainly is no claim to a cognitive-developmental order. The teacher does not need to begin with the altered text activities and end with the poetry-in-response-to-prose activities. But, the activities are generally in ascending order of complexity of articulation. When introducing students to aesthetic response activities, it may be best to begin with unarticulated response to build students' confidence in their abilities and set teacher expectations.

The activities presented throughout focus specifically on aesthetic responses to texts, not the entire range of response possible in the literature curriculum. The larger context of the response-centered curriculum is explored in two equally useful books, *Response and Analysis* by Robert Probst (1988) and *How Porcupines Make Love II* by Alan Purves, et al. (1990). Complementary to Corcoran and Evans's book *Readers, Texts, Teachers,* previously cited, two recent collections of writings by reader-response theorists examining Rosenblatt's work, entitled *The Experience of Reading* and *Transactions with Literature,* provide some useful perspectives for developing a response-centered curriculum (Clifford, 1991; Farrell and Squire, 1990).

Also, textual analysis and efferent reading do belong on the instructional agenda for the literature curriculum. And there is certainly room for transactional writing in the literature curriculum as well. The NCTE TRIP booklet *Writing about Literature* by Kahn, Walter, and Johannessen provides an excellent approach to analysis and argument (1984). But the activities in that book are not substitutes for aesthetic reading and poetic discourse response. Aesthetic reading and responding in poetic discourse should be equally accounted for in the literature curriculum.

The use of poetic discourse for response is not meant as a substitute for a creative writing curriculum either. The poetic discourse activities delineated earlier serve literature aims; much more structure would be necessary to meet the aims of the composition curriculum. The poetic discourse response, however, can serve as prewriting for future poetic writing, as well as stand by itself as a literary response. In both cases the student is engaging in important, and necessary, language activity.

Finally, and this bears repeating, the activities presented here are not intended to follow basic comprehension exercises, nor are they expected to be completed after the textual analysis is over. Both situations may circumvent, and probably undermine, the suggested activities and their intended aims. Response and analysis in school literature instruction are both essential, and they are equally important. Nonetheless, English class may be the only class emphasizing the aesthetic response end of the spectrum. Students receive plenty of analytical and efferent opportunities in their other classes. On the other hand, given that aesthetic reading and aesthetic forms of rationality are not restricted to literary reading or even English teaching, an across-the-curriculum approach to aesthetic reading might be most appropriate.

But mostly, an aesthetic emphasis in reading and responding is meant to reinforce aesthetic language experience as the primary domain of the English language arts. Some recent suggestions made for interdisciplinary curricula appear to treat literature as historical documents to be gleaned for political or sociological evidence, or for ethical truth. Aesthetic approaches seek to treat literature first as an artistic experience for the reader, and only secondarily as a puzzle or a parable. Aesthetic models are as essential for readers of children's literature who might be using efferent basal reading models as for readers who believe they can find all the answers to the meaning of "Heart of Darkness" in *Cliffs Notes*.

Aesthetic approaches also do not preclude any of the traditional approaches to literary criticism. All critical approaches may be used with an aesthetic approach, whether humanistic-ethical, structuralist, deconstructionist, or any other which may appear in the future. Critical approaches all depend on the reader's first experiencing the text as a work of art, even if it is to expose the ideology of art.

Finally, because standardized testing is such an important part of curriculum development, evaluation schemes for literature study must include aesthetic response as one of the activities. Elliot Eisner believes that the "short-term and the instrumental" focus of testing, and the prevalence of testing in schools, is one of the primary reasons for the devaluation of aesthetic knowing in schools (Eisner, 1985, p. 34). As Purves has suggested, a mediating (or medial) activity that focuses on the initial aesthetic response may be essential in producing a true picture of a reader's ability to respond (Purves, 1990). The initial aesthetic response is also crucial data for describing the complexity of the reader's understanding. The necessary expectation for aesthetic response and the activity base for encouraging it, must be part of the curriculum, instruction, and evaluation of English teaching.

Works Cited

Adams, P. (1987). Writing from reading—"Dependent authorship" as a response. In B. Corcoran & E. Evans (Eds.), *Readers, texts, teachers* (pp. 119–152). Upper Montclair, NJ: Boynton/Cook.

Anderson, P. M. (1988). Enhancing aesthetic reading and response to poetry. In R. Blake (Ed.), *Reading, writing, and interpreting literature: Positions and pedagogy* (pp. 138–150). Albany: New York State English Council.

Anderson, P. M. (1990). *Evaluative response to poetic convention at four grade levels.* (ERIC Document Reproduction Service No. ED 314 749.)

Applebee, A. N. (1977). ERIC/RCS report: The elements of response to a literary work: What we have learned. *Research in the Teaching of English, 11,* 255–271.

Applebee, A. N. (1978). *The child's concept of story: Ages two to seventeen.* Chicago: University of Chicago Press.

Applebee, A. N. (1985). Studies in the spectator role: An approach to response to literature. In C. R. Cooper (Ed.), *Researching response to literature and the teaching of literature: Points of departure* (pp. 87–102). Norwood, NJ: Ablex.

Beach, R. (1973). The literary response process of college students. *English Record, 23*(4), 98–116.

Bleich, D. (1975). *Readings and feelings: An introduction to subjective criticism.* Urbana, IL: National Council of Teachers of English.

Bleich, D. (1978). *Subjective criticism.* Baltimore: Johns Hopkins University Press.

Britton, J. (1970). *Language and learning.* Baltimore: Penguin.

Britton, J. (1977). Language and the nature of learning: An individual perspective. In J. R. Squire (Ed.), *The teaching of English* (pp. 1–38). Chicago: National Society for the Study of Education.

Britton, J., Burgess, T., Martin, N., McLeod, A., & Rosen, H. (1975). *The development of writing abilities* (11–18). New York: Macmillan.

Clifford, J. (Ed.) (1991). *The experience of reading: Louise Rosenblatt and reader-response theory.* Portsmouth, NH: Boynton/Cook/Heinemann.

Corcoran, B. (1987). Teachers creating readers. In B. Corcoran & E. Evans (Eds.), *Readers, texts, teachers* (pp. 41–74). Upper Montclair, NJ: Boynton/Cook.

Corcoran, B., & Evans, E. (Eds.) (1987). *Readers, texts, teachers.* Upper Montclair, NJ: Boynton/Cook.

Davenport, G. (1987). The scholar as critic. In *Every force evolves a form: Twenty essays* (pp. 84–98). San Francisco: North Point Press.

Davidson, J. L. (Ed.) (1988). *Counterpoint and beyond: A response to* Becoming a nation of readers. Urbana, IL: National Council of Teachers of English.

Dias, P. (1987). *Making sense of poetry: Patterns in the process.* Ottawa: Canadian Council of Teachers of English.

Early, M. (1977). Reading in the secondary school. In J. R. Squire (Ed.), *The teaching of English* (pp. 189–196). Chicago: National Society for the Study of Education.

Eisner, E. (1985). Aesthetic modes of knowing. In E. Eisner (Ed.), *Learning and teaching the ways of knowing* (pp. 23–36). Chicago: University of Chicago Press.

Evans, E. (1987). Readers recreating texts. In B. Corcoran & E. Evans (Eds.), *Readers, texts, teachers* (pp. 22–40). Upper Montclair, NJ: Boynton/Cook.

Farrell, E. J., & Squire, J. R. (1990). *Transactions with literature: A fifty-year perspective.* Urbana, IL: National Council of Teachers of English.

Galda, S. L. (1982). Assessment: Responses to literature. In A. Berger & H. A. Robinson (Eds.), *Secondary school reading: What research reveals for classroom practice* (pp. 111–125). Urbana, IL: National Conference on Research in English and ERIC Clearinghouse on Reading and Communication Skills.

Gardner, H. (1982). *Art, mind, and brain: A cognitive approach to creativity.* New York: Basic Books.

Golden, J. M., & Guthrie, J. T. (1986). Convergence and divergence in reader response to literature. *Reading Research Quarterly, 21,* 408–421.

Greene, M. (1981). Aesthetic literacy in general education. In J. F. Soltis (Ed.), *Philosophy and education* (pp. 115–141). Chicago: University of Chicago Press.

Greene, M. (1982). Literacy for what? *Phi Delta Kappan, 63,* 326–329.

Hansson, G. (1973). Some types of research on response to literature. *Research in the Teaching of English, 7,* 260–284.

Hansson, G. (1985). Verbal scales in research on response to literature. In C. R. Cooper (Ed.), *Researching response to literature and the teaching of literature: Points of departure* (pp. 212–232). Norwood, NJ: Ablex.

Hirsch, E. D., Jr. (1988). *Cultural literacy: What every American needs to know* (rev. ed.). New York: Random House.

Holland, N. N. (1990). *Holland's guide to psychoanalytic psychology and literature-and-psychology.* New York: Oxford University Press.

Hynds, S. (1989). Bringing life to literature and literature to life: Social constructs and contexts of four adolescent readers. *Research in the Teaching of English, 23,* 30–61.

Iser, W. (1978). *The act of reading: A theory of aesthetic response.* Baltimore: Johns Hopkins University Press.

Kahn, E., Walter, C., & Johannessen, L. (1984). *Writing about literature.* Urbana, IL: ERIC/NCTE.

Koch, K. (1990). *Rose, where did you get that red? Teaching great poetry to children* (Vintage ed. with a new introduction by the author). New York: Random House.

Langer, J. A. (1990). The process of understanding: Reading for literary and informative purposes. *Research in the Teaching of English, 24,* 229–260.

Long, S. A., Winograd, P. N., & Bridge, C. A. (1989). The effects of reader and text characteristics on imagery reported during and after reading. *Reading Research Quarterly, 24,* 353–372.

Miall, D. S. (1985). The structure of response: A repertory grid study of a poem. *Research in the Teaching of English, 19,* 254–268.

Nell, V. (1988). The psychology of reading for pleasure: Needs and gratifications. *Reading Research Quarterly, 23,* 6–50.

Osgood, C. E., Suci, G. J., & Tannenbaum, P. H. (1957). *The measurement of meaning.* Urbana, IL: University of Illinois Press.

Paivio, A. (1986). *Mental representations: A dual coding approach.* New York: Oxford University Press.

Petrosky, A. R. (1985). Response: A way of knowing. In C. R. Cooper (Ed.), *Researching response to literature and the teaching of literature: Points of departure* (pp. 70–83). Norwood, NJ: Ablex.

Probst, R. (1988). *Response and analysis: Teaching literature in the junior and senior high school.* Portsmouth, NH: Boynton/Cook/Heinemann.

Purves, A. C. (1979). That sunny dome: Those caves of ice: A model for research in reader response. *College English, 40,* 802–812.

Purves, A. C. (1985). That sunny dome: Those caves of ice. In C. R. Cooper (Ed.), *Researching response to literature and the teaching of literature: Points of departure* (pp. 54–69). Norwood, NJ: Ablex.

Purves, A. C. (1990, November). *How tests can support the process of literary understanding.* Paper presented at the meeting of the National Council of Teachers of English, Atlanta, GA.

Purves, A. C., & Beach, R. (1972). *Literature and the reader: Research in response to literature, reading interests, and the teaching of literature.* Urbana, IL: National Council of Teachers of English.

Purves, A. C., & Niles, O. (1984). The challenge to education to produce literate citizens. In A. C. Purves & O. Niles (Eds.), *Becoming readers in a complex society* (pp. 1–15). Chicago: National Society for the Study of Education.

Purves, A. C., with Rippere, V. (1968). *Elements of writing about a literary work: A study of response to literature* (NCTE Research Report No. 9). Champaign, IL: National Council of Teachers of English.

Purves, A. C., with Harnisch, D. L., Quirk, D. L., & Bauer, B. (1981). *Reading and literature: American achievement in international perspective.* Urbana, IL: National Council of Teachers of English.

Purves, A. C., Rogers, T., & Soter, A. O. (1990). *How porcupines make love II: Teaching a response-centered literature curriculum.* New York: Longman.

Richards, I. A. (1962). *Practical criticism.* (Original work published 1929). New York: Harcourt, Brace & World.

Rivlin, A. (1974). *Poetry unfolding.* Madison, WI: Knowledge Unlimited.

Rosenblatt, L. M. (1983). *Literature as exploration* (4th ed.). New York: MLA.

Rosenblatt, L. M. (1978). *The reader, the text, the poem: The transactional theory of the literary work.* Carbondale: Southern Illinois University Press.

Rosenblatt, L. M. (1980). "What facts does this poem teach you?" *Language Arts, 57,* 386–394.

Rosenblatt, L. M. (1985). Viewpoints: Transaction versus interaction—A terminological rescue operation. *Research in the Teaching of English, 19,* 96–107.

Rubano, G. L., & Anderson, P. M. (1988). Reasoning and writing with metaphors. *English Journal, 77*(8), 34–37.

Sadoski, M. (1984). Text structure, imagery, and affect in the recall of a story by children. In J. A. Niles & L. A. Harris (Eds.), *Changing perspectives in research in reading/language processing and instruction: Thirty-third yearbook of the National Reading Conference* (pp. 48–53). Rochester, NY: National Reading Conference.

Sadoski, M., Goetz, E. T., & Kangiser, S. (1988). Imagination in story response: Relationships between imagery, affect, and structural importance. *Reading Research Quarterly, 23,* 320–336.

Squire, J. R. (1964). *The responses of adolescents while reading four short stories* (NCTE Research Report No. 2). Champaign, IL: National Council of Teachers of English.

Squire, J. R. (1989, November). *Research on reader response and the national literature initiative.* Paper presented at the meeting of the National Council of Teachers of English: Baltimore.

Squire, J. R. (Ed.). (1968). *Response to literature.* Urbana, IL: National Council of Teachers of English.

Suleiman, S. R., & Crosman, I. (Eds.) (1980). *The reader in the text: Essays on audience and interpretation.* Princeton, NJ: Princeton University Press.

Sunstein, B. S., & Anderson, P. M. (1989). Metaphor, science, and the spectator role. *Teaching English in the Two-Year College, 16*(1), 9–16.

Tompkins, J. P. (Ed.). (1980). *Reader-response criticism.* Baltimore: Johns Hopkins University Press.

Vygotsky, L. (1962). *Thought and language.* Cambridge: MIT Press.

Authors

Philip M. Anderson is associate professor in the Department of Secondary Education and Youth Services at Queens College of the City University of New York. He began his career as a language arts and reading teacher at Parkview High School in Orford-ville, Wisconsin. After supervising student teachers at the University of Wisconsin–Madison, where he received a Ph.D. in curriculum and instruction, he taught in the English Department at Ohio University and the Education Department at Brown University. He is the author or coauthor of over thirty articles and chapters. In 1989 he was presented the Charles Swain Thomas Distinguished Service Award by the New England Association of Teachers of English.

Gregory Rubano teaches English at Toll Gate High School in Warwick, Rhode Island. During 1978–85, he was also a methods associate in the Master of Arts in Teaching program at Brown University. He received a B.A. from William and Mary, an M.A.T. from Brown, and currently is completing a Ph.D. in curriculum and instruction at the University of Connecticut. In 1986 he was selected an NEH Fellow for Independent Study in the Humanities, and from 1987 to 1991 he was a member of the Test of Standard Written English Committee for Educational Testing Service.